THE CONTEMPORARY CHRISTIAN

IS VOLUME

134

OF THE

Twentieth Century Encyclopedia of Catholicism

UNDER SECTION

XIV

OUTSIDE THE CHURCH

IT IS ALSO THE

140TH

VOLUME IN ORDER OF PUBLICATION

Edited by HENRI DANIEL-ROPS of the Académie Française

THE CONTEMPORARY CHRISTIAN

By THOMAS CORBISHLEY, S.J.

80490

HAWTHORN BOOKS · PUBLISHERS · *New York*

First Edition, January, 1967

NIHIL OBSTAT

Ioannes M. T. Barton, S.T.D., C.S.S.

Censor Deputatus

IMPRIMATUR

Patritius Casey

Vicarius Generalis

Westmonasterii, die XXV NOVEMBRIS MCMLXV

9472

CONTENTS

PART I

THE CHRISTIAN AS HUMANIST

CHAPTER I

THE CHALLENGE OF HUMANISM

One of the most fascinating, as it is one of the most difficult of problems, is the analysis of the processes by which human beings advance in knowledge. Even in the simplest developments, the acquisition of the most ordinary items of information, what we might call horizontal progress, profoundly mysterious factors are at work to enable us to learn the most elementary truths. Perhaps the most rudimentary example we can quote is that of learning the multiplication table. Even the child who will persist in thinking that $7 \times 7 = 47$ has already performed a remarkable feat of imaginative classification, even to get the answer wrong. The really astonishing thing is to be able to get an answer at all, to recognize that "7 times 7" has a meaning and is not just a silly noise.

Or pause for a moment to reflect on the remark of the small girl who was taken for the first time to see a pigsty, and who, as she watched its denizens snuffling and rooting about their trough, said: "Oh, now I know why they are called pigs." Not a very clever or precocious statement; but, again, if we stop to think, we shall realize what a complex and flexible apparatus must lie behind and render possible the experience and reflections which led up to that declaration.

But if we turn to examine man's growth in depth of understanding, vertical growth, as it were, we are confronted with a situation which baffles description and defies analysis. We need not for the moment think of the profound discoveries of the great thinkers of mankind but of the ordinary interchange of ideas between normal, simple people. Take the following sentence which I read recently: "Whether you smoke or not is your business." It requires no special ability to understand the implications of such a remark; it is the sort of thing people are saying everywhere and every day. Yet it implies a considerable degree of what one may call moral as well as intellectual sophistication to formulate or to appreciate it. It presupposes no small amount of social dialogue, experience of human habits, of their medical effects, their impact on other people and so on.

Extend this sort of treatment to the whole field of what we call philosophy, logic and metaphysics, ethics and psychology, to the field of human history, to the world of politics, to the discoveries of science, to the realm of religion, and you begin to realize how all but infinite is the complex of man's thought. This vast universe of ideas, opinions, judgements, guesses, beliefs, hopes and fears has grown up for the last five to ten thousand years, largely under the influence of mutual interchange, embodied in tradition, modified by changing experience. Advances have been made, often under the impact of the teaching or inspiration of some man of genius; at times there has been what looked like stagnation, at other times there have been rapid advances. Not infrequently an almost head-on collision between rival theories or doctrines has produced an unexpected result, which is much more than a synthesis of the two.

It has seemed desirable to draw attention in this way to something which is, in itself, almost too obvious to need such emphasis, because the attitude of mind which goes under the name of contemporary philosophy has done such a disservice to human thought by its trivial and irresponsible treatment of it. To base a whole system of belief on what is little better than an exercise in grammatical analysis is to cheapen and debase the rich coinage of man's reason. In any excursion into the world of human experience, it behoves us to observe a decent humility and a sense of reverence. Only so shall we hope to do anything like justice to a reality of surpassing significance.

On the basis of such considerations as these, it should be made quite clear from the outset that the movement which calls itself Humanism is one with which, in principle, no Christian need have any quarrel. On the contrary, the Humanists earn our gratitude for recalling us to some aspects of the truth which some of us were in danger of ignoring or, at least, not taking seriously enough. At the same time, it seems not unreasonable to suggest that the quarrel which has arisen is not entirely of our seeking. All too often, the humanist has misunderstood, misrepresented and then proceeded to pour scorn on what is alleged to be the Christian view of life. Thus, in his book *A Challenge to Christianity,* Mr J. B. Coates writes as follows:

> In her *Testament of Social Science* Barbara Wootton describes the Christian attitude in face of the advance of humanism and science in the modern period as one of continual retreat. Christianity has put up a resistance, indeed, but it has been that of an army fighting a rearguard action and abandoning one position after another. If today Christianity does not find itself in conflict with natural sciences it is because religion no longer dares to say anything about the behaviour of natural phenomena, having been always proved wrong when it did so. But today, Mrs Wootton remarks, Christianity is being systematically driven from the spiritual sphere also, by developments in psychology and the social sciences. In view of the work of Freud and the great progress in anthropology, it is becoming increasingly difficult to interpret the phenomena of morality and the religious consciousness in terms of the intervention of grace and a personal relationship with a transcendent God. We have so far seen only the first skirmishes in the battle between religion and the social sciences, but Mrs Wootton cannot believe that the Church will have any alternative in the long run, in its interpretation of religious experience, but to retreat again, to argue that, just as God controls the behaviour of atoms through the laws of physics, so he controls mental processes through the laws of physiology and psychology. She comes then to the conclusion that before long

Christianity will no longer have any territory within its grasp, that science, in a word, will take over and achieve a total victory, the "superstition" of Christianity being finally routed.[1]

Well, we have all heard the story of the small child, looking at a picture of the early Christian martyrs in the arena and feeling sorry for the poor lion that hadn't got a Christian, but nobody has ever suggested that it was really the Christians who persecuted the Romans. The foregoing passage does really seem to mean—if words mean anything—that humanism has set out to abolish Christianity. To interpret this as meaning that Christianity has therefore picked a quarrel with humanism seems to be going a bit too far. *Cet animal est très méchant; quand on l'attaque, il se défend.* If Christianity has found itself at war with humanism, the war is not one of its choosing. Or perhaps Lady Wootton thinks that the very existence of Christianity constitutes a "permanent state of aggression" against humanism, rather as the very existence of an independent Goa was described by the Indian Foreign Minister. But this is hardly the language of cold reason.

What the following chapters propose to do is to examine the contemporary scene in the light of this tension between two systems of ideas, to see how and why the clash between them has arisen, to suggest that the quarrel is largely unreal and unnecessary, and finally to show that, far from being mutually hostile, the two systems are substantially in agreement, that each needs the other to complement it. I am not a scientist, but as far as I can understand what the physicists say, there have been developed two systems for interpreting natural phenomena, the Newtonian and the relativist. So far as I know, it is not suggested that Einstein has refuted or replaced Newton. He has argued that the Newtonian world provides the basis for a more general interpretation of natural phenomena, but not that relativity has "conquered" the previous way of looking at things. One can understand Newton,

[1] J. B. Coates, *A Challenge to Christianity*, London, Watts, 1958, p. 126.

without having to accept or to understand Einstein; one comes to Einstein through Newton.

It seems fair to suggest that the relation between Humanism and Christianity is analogous to that between Newton and Einstein. Humanism explains the world in an adequate way, within its own limits; and, for its purposes, does not need to go beyond its findings. But it remains partial and incomplete as a picture of total reality, which is presented to us by the Christian faith. You cannot be a Christian without also being, in the positive sense, a Humanist; you may be a Humanist without feeling the need of the fuller truth of Christianity.

But if this is so, how are we to explain the great divide, the cleavage that has arisen between these two systems of ideas which both claim adherents who are often high-minded, sincere, not lacking in intelligence and, in many ways, indistinguishable from each other in their attitudes to the daily business of life? To answer this question at all adequately calls for the analysis of a number of factors so great as to be beyond the capacity of any one individual, certainly within the scope of a few brief chapters. But it is possible to separate out four main strands, though they are in practice so intertwined that the study of them in isolation is necessarily misleading.

The four strands, then, may be labelled respectively the metaphysical, the historical, the temperamental and the moral. By the metaphysical I mean the state of affairs which results from the division of reality into the spiritual and the material. For, despite the obvious fact that the material only makes sense to, and therefore derives its meaning from, the spiritual, from reason or intelligence, the generality of men fall easy victims to the notion that the spiritual is somehow less real than the material. The concrete, the here and now, the felt presence—these are what most appeal to us creatures of flesh and blood.

"This warm, kind world is all I know." The poet's words find an easy and sympathetic response in the hearts of all of us. The Apostle may declare that faith gives substance to our hopes, makes us certain of realities we do not see; but we remain, often enough, unsure and unconvinced.

When, therefore, we encounter a doctrine which seems to promise us a complete system without any need of a world beyond this one, when this system is linked so closely and so directly with the scientific mentality which, whatever else we may say about it, does get things done, does deliver the goods; when we see the whole scientific pattern growing in range and richness in an almost dramatic fashion, while the traditional religious picture calls for constant restatement and what may look like continual impoverishment; then, it is hardly surprising that a large number of men should come to think that a bird in the hand is worth a whole covey below the horizon.

It is this metaphysical condition which makes possible the historical developments which have led up to the present situation. Contemporary humanism, described by Sir Julian Huxley as: "This new idea-system, whose birth we of the mid-twentieth century are witnessing" [2] is not, of course, as modern in origin as all that. We may indeed apply to it the words of the preacher: "Never man calls a thing new, but it is something already known to the ages that went before us; only we have no record of older days. So, believe me, the fame of tomorrow's doings will be forgotten by men of a later time." [3] We have, in fact, enough records of older days to know that, even in the days of the Psalmist, "The fool said in his own heart: 'There is no God'." The Humanist attitude to religion in general has much in common with that of Epicurus; its attitude to Christianity was, to no small extent, already propounded by Celsus before the end of the second century; Augustine and Aquinas were both fully aware of the problem raised by the sceptical mentality which lies behind Humanism, and, though the scale of the problem is perhaps greater today and the solution calls for greater precision of statement,

[2] *The Humanist Frame,* edited by Julian Huxley, Allen & Unwin, 1961, p. 14.
[3] Eccles. 1. 10, 11.

there does not appear to be anything radically novel in the nature of the problem itself.

But, for Sir Julian Huxley, it all began with the *Origin of Species*. As he says himself: "The idea of evolution kindled my imagination while I was still at school." [4] Since then he has organized his thinking more and more round this central point. He has come to see what he rightly calls the "knowledge-explosion of the last hundred years" as "providing man with a new revelation, a new vision of his destiny".[5] Finally, it issued in the general doctrine, the "unified framework of ideas", called by him "Evolutionary Humanism":

> The implications of this integrated idea-system seemed fairly satisfactory. It related every kind of human activity to the yardstick of desirable evolutionary direction. It related individual and community within the frame of the continuing psycho-social process. It reconciled "mind" and "matter" in a dual-aspect monism, and put all phenomena, cosmological and biological, material and human, short-term and long-term, into relation with the embracing process of evolution. In its light man's higher activities, of science, art and religion, appeared, not as independent entities but as interlocking functions of our evolving species. It showed that all general concepts such as *justice* or *phlogiston, atom* or *soul,* are best regarded as mechanisms for ordering and handling our experience—as hypotheses which must be checked against experience and either adjusted and elaborated (as with *justice* and *atom*) or rejected (as with *phlogiston*) or transcended (as with *soul*). It could provide an all-inclusive aim for the human species, in the shape of greater fulfilment through increased realization of possibilities.[6]

So far, so good. It is difficult to share the exuberant optimism of Sir Julian; but in principle there is nothing to object to in his statement.

The next two sentences, alas, cannot be accepted entirely at their face value, though even here one can largely sympathize with Sir Julian's approach:

[4] *The Humanist Frame,* p. 5.
[5] *Ibid.,* p. 6.
[6] *Ibid.,* p. 6.

It assigned man to his proper place in nature, and showed him his true destiny. It was not a rigid system of dogmas, resistant or impervious to change; it was an open system, capable of indefinite further development. Above all it could give reassurance to all those searching for some firm ground of belief and moral direction in the violence and disorder of contemporary existence.[7]

Some of this will call for clarification at a later stage, but the immediate question it raises is why Sir Julian should think that this ideal is one which need bring him into serious conflict with believing Christians.

The complete answer to this question must wait for the next chapter; but the short historical answer is that the supposed conflict is due to two main causes; one, the failure on the part of some scientists and some theologians to delimit carefully their own respective fields of intellectual activity; two, the fact that theologians as a body have been too uncertain in their minds about the precise purpose of theology and, it may be, too reluctant to concede to others the personal primacy which they once enjoyed.

Which brings us to the third and fourth of the strands—the temperamental and the moral. It is not irrelevant to suggest that there is such a thing as a scientific temperament; that, just as there are men who like "messing about in boats" so there are men who like messing about in laboratories or tinkering with machines. Rudyard Kipling, in a poem entitled *The Sons of Martha,* describes them thus:

> It is their care in all the ages to take the buffet and cushion the shock;
> It is their care that the gear engages; it is their care that the switches lock . . .
> They finger death at their gloves' end, where they piece and repiece the living wires:
> He rears against the gates they tend; they feed him hungry behind their fires . . .

As contrasted with them are the natural contemplatives, the philosophers, the mystics especially, but all those who

[7] *Ibid.,* p. 6.

prefer to speculate rather than to operate. (Few men, in fact, are wholly one or the other; but as a rough division it will do.) They are the sons of Mary as described in the final stanza of Kipling's poem:

> And the sons of Mary smile and are blessed—they know the angels are on their side.
> They know in them is the Grace confessed, and for them are the Mercies multiplied.
> They sit at the Feet, they hear the Word; they see how truly the Promise runs:
> They have cast their burden upon the Lord—and the Lord he lays it on Martha's sons.

Temperamentally diverse or not, scientists and theologians are regrettably alike in that they share certain moral weaknesses. They have their little vanities, their little blindnesses to the achievements of others, their little jealousies. It is true that, by profession, the theologians ought to set an example of disinterested devotion to absolute truth for its own sake. But it must be confessed that they are not all impeccable. It is not without significance that the term *odium theologicum* was invented many years ago. It is possible to suspect that scientists too are not without their professional pride, and would not be reluctant to take over the role which, for centuries, was played by the theologians.

There, then, seem to be the roots of disagreement between the new orthodoxy of Humanism and the older orthodoxy of Christian faith. It is time now to turn and examine more precisely the terms of the challenge which Humanism has thrown down to the Christian believer.

We have already seen two or three passages from prominent Humanists which will have given some idea of the major gravamina of their charges against Christianity. The most important of them is that the Christian conception of God, of man's relation to God and of the rôle of grace in Christian life is such as to diminish man's responsibility for his destiny and, in effect, so to concentrate man's attention on the next world as to inhibit him from bestirring himself as he should about the affairs of this world.

Thus Sir Julian Huxley, while admitting that "science can become the ally of religion instead of its rival or enemy", makes it quite clear, as does Lady Wootton, that Christianity has had its day and that he understands religion in a strangely irreligious way.

> All theistic religions, he asserts, are based on the God hypothesis (or to use Ralph Turner's more inclusive term, the daimonic hypothesis)—the belief that there exist supernatural beings of a personal or super-personal nature, capable of influencing natural events, including events in human minds. This is a dualistic theory, for it implies the existence of a basic and essential cleavage between natural and supernatural realms of being. . . . A theological system incorporating such beliefs has a number of consequences which Humanists find undesirable. The belief in supernatural beings capable of affecting human destiny leads to petitionary rather than aspirational prayer. . . . Belief in a supernatural afterlife leads to concentration on attaining salvation in the other world and to a lack of concern for life in this world and its possible improvement. . . . Belief in the value of orthodox Christian beliefs and practices as the sole or main means of achieving salvation leads to the rejection or playing down of other ideas as to what constitutes "salvation", and of other methods of transcending selfhood. . . . Above all belief in an omnipotent, omniscient and omnibenevolent God leads to a frustrating dilemma at the very heart of our approach to reality. For many thinking people it is incompatible with our knowledge of nature and history and with the facts of suffering, evil and human misery.[8]

He has already said that man must face his future

> unaided by outside help. In the evolutionary pattern of thought there is no longer need or room for the supernatural. The earth was not created; it evolved. So did all the animals and plants that inhabit it, including our human selves, mind and soul as well as brain. So did religion. Religions are organs of psychosocial man concerned with human destiny and with experiences of sacredness and transcendence. . . . In their

[8] *The Humanist Frame*, pp. 38-40.

evolution, some (but by no means all) have given birth to the concepts of gods as supernatural beings endowed with mental and spiritual properties and capable of intervening in the affairs of nature, including man. These theistic religions are organs of human thought in its interaction with the puzzling complex world with which it has to contend—the outer world of nature and the inner world of man's own nature. In this, they resemble other early organizations of human thought confronted with nature, like the doctrine of the Four Elements, earth, air, fire, water, or the Eastern concept of rebirth and reincarnation. Like these they are destined to disappear in competition with other, truer and more embracing thought-organizations which are handling the same range of raw or processed experience.[9]

Clearly there is a whole lot of question-begging going on here, which will call for careful examination later. For the present we must allow Sir Julian to expound his objections to certain specifically Christian doctrines.

Christian theology calls itself monotheistic, but permits itself a partial-polytheism in the doctrine of the Trinity, while the position ascribed to the Virgin, the Angels and the Saints in Catholicism and to a lesser degree in other sects, gives full rein to polydaimonism. Christian theology bases itself on revelation and on belief in the historical reality of supernatural events such as the incarnation and resurrection of Jesus as the Son of God. . . . Belief in the fall of man and the necessity of redemption through an incarnate divine Saviour has led to the cruel (and untrue) doctrines of Original Sin and damnation for unbelievers, as well as a belief in the guilt and inherent inferiority of the female sex.[10]

Not that Sir Julian objects to theology, but it must be what he calls scientific theology. He has little use for the claim of theology, in the old sense, to be a science, still less to be the queen of sciences. If theology is to be truly scientific it must adopt scientific methods.

Man's religious aim must be to achieve not a static but a dynamic spiritual equilibrium. And his emergent religion must

[9] *The Humanist Frame,* pp. 18-19.
[10] *Ibid.*

therefore learn how to be an open and self-correcting system like that of his science. . . . Religious concepts like God, incarnation, the soul, salvation, original sin, grace, atonement, all have a basis in man's experience of phenomenal reality. It is necessary now to analyse that basis of reality into its component parts, and then to reassemble these elements, together with any new factors that have come to light, into concepts which correspond more closely to reality and are more relevant to present circumstances. . . . It should be possible to reformulate such ideas as Divine Law, obedience to God's Will, or union with the mind of God, in an evolutionary terminology consonant with existing scientific knowledge. Again Christian ethics (to which the world owes a great debt) are based on the doctrine of Original Sin resulting from the Fall of Man. This attempts to give an intelligible interpretation of such general and well-nigh universal phenomena as our sense of guilt, our search for atonement, our authoritarian conscience, our rigorous sense of right and wrong, our consequent persecution of those who deviate from what we feel is the right path. . . . Reformation—even reappraisal—is perhaps most necessary in regard to man's inner life and what, for want of a better terminology, is called spiritual development.[11]

Manifestly, from the foregoing passage, the challenge of Humanism is by no means a negative and destructive one, and it is possible to show and perhaps to persuade the Humanist to see that his criticisms of traditional religious formularies are not so devastating as he appears to think, that, as so often happens, our apparent enemies turn out to be friends in disguise, in that they compel us to re-examine our own ideas and our traditional ways of talking about them, in such a way that we come to understand them better ourselves, and are therefore in a better position to explain them to others.

Not unnaturally it is the apparent or alleged inhumanity of Christian teaching which chiefly irks the Humanist. Thus Morris Ginsberg, preaching the gospel of progress, declares:

Faith in progress on the road to a universal high civilization can be restored if it can be shown to be a reasonable faith. Is this secular faith in conflict with the older faiths of traditional religion, particularly the Christian faith? Yes, if it belongs to

[11] *The Humanist Frame*, pp. 43-5.

the Christian faith to "sit loose to civilization". That is the test. The Humanist is reconciled to reality and makes his home there, and has a horror of the black-and-white fantasy of heaven and hell. . . . A new Humanist ethic is needed, to create in the climate of modern ideals and in the context of new possibilities an ethos of personal excellence and public spirit worthy of the human vocation, the ethos of an enlightened and universal civilization.[12]

The really sad thing about this kind of pleading is not that it presents us with an ideal that is unacceptable or indeed particularly novel, but that we Christians should somehow have created the idea that it is out of harmony with Christian teaching. Without anticipating the argument of the next chapter, it may be as well to interject here the remark that we clearly need to examine our consciences to see where and how we have failed to live up to our own high principles. For here we have a group of men who are lacking neither in intelligence nor in knowledge and who yet seem to be convinced that they are bringing to the notice of mankind a doctrine which is unheard of. Whose fault is it, if Aldous Huxley can speak as follows? "Religions, even the highest of them, consist at most times and in most places, of one part of spirituality to nine of superstition, magic, priestcraft and bad science." What are we to make of his wholesale condemnation of the traditional efforts to train men to right conduct?

Oddly enough, nobody ever tells us *how* to be good. None of the child's pastors and masters ever offers to teach him a practical way of implementing his New Year's resolutions, of actualizing his potential virtues. "For the good that I would do I do not; but the evil which I would do not, that I do." St Paul's problem is everybody's problem. How is it to be solved? Experience shows that bribes and threats, that punishments and rewards, that good intentions and efforts of will are, all of them, only moderately effective. . . . Even systematic conditioning has failed up till now to produce the results expected of it. The Jesuits boasted that by their educational methods they could condition any child into life-long obedience to the Church. But Voltaire was one of their star pupils, and the

[12] *The Humanist Frame*, p. 141.

moral level of those who have received a religious education is not conspicuously higher than those whose education has been in secular schools. Modern dictators have borrowed freely from the Jesuits, have improved their methods and have engendered in their subjects a greater degree of orthodoxy than was achieved even in the palmiest days of the Counter-Reformation. But imposed orthodoxy offers no solution to our ethical problems. . . .[13]

Ignoring the remarks about the Jesuits' boast and the offensive comparison of our methods of education with the indoctrination of their subjects by modern dictators, we may well admit that this problem of the comparative failure of Christians to produce a noticeably higher standard of moral conduct than their neighbours is a real one and must induce in us some honest searchings of heart. True, while quoting St Paul's words, Mr Huxley does not complete the passage, by reminding us that the Apostle finds that, with the grace of God, he can succeed in overcoming himself. The Humanist is not likely to take that answer seriously. Yet it is one aspect of our general problem which calls for close and critical investigation.

But even worse, not only are Christians not noticeably superior to their fellows; they are considerably inferior. According to Francis Williams, "the history of Christianity is sodden with blood, torture and warfare", though he admits that "rival Christians" have now settled down to live with each other "after trying to kill each other for so long".[14] Lady Wootton, however, in asserting that "the Humanist is against hunger, poverty, ignorance, cruelty and bloodshed" seems to imply that we Christians, because we use "arguments . . . derived from religious dogmas, or that rest solely upon appeals to the will of God" are apparently indifferent to these human miseries.[15] Again, one must ask, how *can* we have given this impression?

It is high time to conclude this inevitably selective analysis

[13] *The Humanist Frame*, pp. 427-8.
[14] *Ibid.*, p. 98.
[15] *Ibid.*, p. 348

of the Humanist challenge. But if it has been selective, it has tried to be representative. Precisely because we claim that the Humanist attack on Christianity rests on a misconception, we must be as careful as possible to make sure that we are not misconceiving or misrepresenting the Humanist's own position. That is why it is preferable to quote rather than to summarize or interpret. Perhaps we may add one final quotation, again from Lady Wootton:

> Nothing perhaps separates this century so sharply from its immediate predecessor as the loss amongst educated men and women of the conviction of the literal truth of the basic dogmas of the Christian religion and of the certainty of individual survival after death. As a result of this loss, a tremendous, though generally silent, shift has occurred in the bases of morality. We ask no longer what is pleasing to God but what is good for man.[16]

"We ask no longer what is pleasing to God but what is good for man." Here, it would seem, is the crux of our problem. The manifest implication of the sentence is that there is some necessary conflict between God's good pleasure and man's well-being. Yet surely a religion which holds as its central belief the idea that God himself has, through the incarnation, shared man's own joys and sorrows; which maintains that man is created for an eternity of happiness; which preaches the paramount duty of universal charity; which asserts that man cannot show a greater love than by laying down his life for his fellow-man: such a religion, surely, should not merely welcome the Humanist's ideals but should itself find a welcome in the Humanist's own heart.

[16] *The Humanist Frame,* p. 351.

CHAPTER II

A CHRISTIAN EXAMINATION OF CONSCIENCE

At the heart of the Christian faith and at the origin of the Christian story stands the figure of a man whom Christians believe to be the supreme revelation of God's truth. (We believe him to be, of course, fully divine; but it is with his human function that we are here directly concerned.) In him, we hold, the eternal truth is manifested, and manifested in the most perfect way possible, because of the entire limpidity of his humanity. By this "limpidity" we mean that in him, as man, is found the perfection of human intelligence and of moral excellence. For the understanding of truth, as we know from our experience, demands not only intellectual capacity but also moral integrity. How often have men of great intellectual gifts failed to do full justice to the truth, because of some defect of character, some self-seeking ambition, some lack of moral scruple, some indolence or vanity or greed.

This revelation, made by Christ to his followers, has been committed to his fellow-men, to preserve, to propound, but above all to practise. Yet, since all men are to a greater or less extent opaque where Christ is limpid, the Christian message has at all times been in some degree inadequately expressed, where it has not been grossly distorted. It is this distortion which must now occupy our attention; for it is by appreciating our own failures as Christians that we shall come to an understanding of the Humanists' rejection of our beliefs; we may even be prompted to try to do something to heal the breach.

It is, of course, in the nature of things that we fallible human beings should have proved incapable of living up to the fullness of Christ's truth. "We are," as St Paul reminds us, "no better than pots of earthenware to contain this treasure." But we can scarcely blame others if we have borne such poor witness to the light within us. We are not, for the present, concerned with others' shortcomings, but with our own. And, as Professor Butterfield has recalled, "the cause of morality is really furthered, in so far as a self-judgement has been brought about".[1]

In the vast field of theological writing and human conduct which goes by the name of "Christian", there is, once again, the greatest danger that we may distort the evidence by the necessity of rigid selection. But there are certain obvious ways in which Christians have not merely failed to live up to the fullness of the truth they profess but have actually presented to the world a totally misleading picture of what they ought to stand for. Nor let us plead that not only have Christians from the beginning been misunderstood, but that there is no possibility of our not being misunderstood. True as it may be that Christ foretold that there would always be conflict between his followers and "the world"; true as it may be that, from the beginning, Christian teaching was misrepresented by Jew and Roman alike; true as it may be that the good man, as even Plato recognized, will be persecuted for his very goodness; it yet remains true that the gravest scandal which, down the centuries, the Christian has given to the unbeliever has sprung, not from his virtues, but from his follies and failures. It is of these that we must now speak.

The fundamental objection which the unprejudiced student of Christian history may well bring is that we have shown a strangely ambivalent attitude to the society in which we

[1] *International Conflict in the Twentieth Century,* London, Routledge, Kegan Paul, 1960, p. 23.

have found ourselves at different times. On the one hand, in Morris Ginsberg's phrase we have "sat loose to civilization"; on the other hand, all too often, we have identified ourselves too closely with the defects of a particular culture. While we may understand and, to some extent, excuse the passionate protest against a vicious urban society which drove the Fathers of the Desert out of the cities into the wilderness, while we may plead that, at a later stage in history, the great Benedictine tradition, which was a modified form of that early movement, did in fact prove to be one of the great civilizing forces in Europe, it remains incontestably true that, for whatever reason, the great work of scientific development and material improvement of the human lot in modern times has been the achievement of those who were, on the whole, outside the Christian body.

At the same time, all too often, we have too easily identified Christianity with some particular social or political organization. Ever since the days of Constantine we have too often sought to safeguard the interests of God by sheltering behind the power of Caesar. To quote Herbert Butterfield again:

> Many Christians still allow their thinking to be unconsciously shaped by the memory of that ancient system of privilege. Their minds are still governed by a traditional notion of the part which the Church should play in an organized society and a developing civilization. They expect to have the dice loaded in their favour either by governments or by educational systems or by the continuing power of social convention. In this way, in an important transition period, they reduce their chances of influencing by other means a world with which they are too much at cross purposes. There is nothing in New Testament Christianity which authorizes us to claim from Providence that things should be made easy for us in the way to which the Church has been accustomed. Nothing in religion itself gives us the right to expect that even in the cause of the Gospel we should enjoy the alliance of political authorities, mundane systems, vested interests and organized force. If Christianity has, in some respects, come into a period of decline, one of the primary reasons for this is the fact that at a crucial moment in history it chose to

make this alliance with power, and has clung to it with pathetic consequences for fifteen hundred years. One of the reasons why it contributes less than we might wish to the problems of our time is the fact that its traditional systems of thought have been so intertwined with that mundane order of things which it accepted as its ally. All this has long provoked a profound resentment in well-meaning men, who do not always understand that the Christian faith is not necessarily allied to the regimes and systems to which churchmen have come to attach it. . . . It is better to think of Christianity as it was in the earliest centuries of its history than to be deluded by the kinds of power it has enjoyed in the very long intervening period.[2]

Perhaps at first sight we feel this is an unfair indictment. Is Professor Butterfield really suggesting that the Christian Church in the fourth century should have allowed itself to go on being persecuted, instead of accepting the protection of Imperial Rome? Is it not natural and right that Christians should seek for peace and for the shelter of a benevolent authority to enable them to promote their work for the glory of God? Did not St Paul himself take advantage of his Roman citizenship to make his preaching of the Gospel more unhampered? Have not some of the greatest saints felt justified in making use of their influence with men of wealth and power in order to promote good works of various kinds?

Reasonable enough such a reaction may be. Yet what Professor Butterfield is saying has profoundly important relevance to our present theme. What he is saying is that, justifiable as such conduct may well be, it is not precisely the conduct which we should describe as *specifically* Christian. The great problem, almost, it might be said, the great paradox of Christianity is that, while it must inevitably express itself in outward forms of one sort or another, the very universality of its message means that it cannot be stated in one final and absolute form, that it must be for ever proving its essential independence of the different forms in which, from time to time, it is discovered.

Perhaps we can see this most clearly in the immediate

[2] *Ibid.*, pp. 107-8.

present when we are discovering that one of the great impedi-
ments to the acceptance of Christianity by the younger nations of Africa and Asia is the inevitable yet unfortunate
fact that it is stated so much in terms of Western culture. In
the seventeenth century a great experiment in the adaptation
of the essential Christian message to certain oriental forms
of expression was frustrated by the action of those who
thought of Christianity so much in Western forms of thought
and ritual that they imagined that any attempt at adaptation
was necessarily a betrayal of the essence of Christianity. Yet
Christ's own life was a continual protest against the idea
that the truth of God could be found only within the forms
of Judaism, the traditions of the elders, the minutiae of the
Mosaic Law. At the same time, as he himself said, he had
come not to destroy that Law but to fulfil it. The mystery
and the wonder of the incarnation is that, with no more than
the simple environment of a primitive pastoral society within
which to work, with no better implements than an unsophisticated language and a score of homely illustrations, with a
handful of adherents who would have found it difficult to
get into what we should call today "a good school", he
launched upon the world a movement of such explosive
force that it was not merely to burst the narrow confines of
Judaism but was to prove too powerful for Rome itself to
contain, and, as we are convinced, will endure to the end of
time. Yet its success is not to be measured in the sort of
categories which men normally use to estimate achievement.
Again and again we need to recall that at the heart of the
Christian gospel is that "collision and contradiction" as
Chesterton spoke of the cross; that Christ's kingdom is not
of this world; that, in St Paul's words, "we are the imposters
who speak the truth, the unknown men whom all men know;
dying we still live on; disciplined by suffering we are not
done to death; . . . poor ourselves we bring wealth to many;
penniless we own the world." [3]

We are, therefore, false to our truest selves, in so far as we

[3] 2 Cor. 6. 8-10.

mistake any earthly reality for the essentially hidden thing that the Christian life is. What is more, if we encourage others to identify Christianity with any temporal way of life or culture or any other man-made organization, we inevitably lead them to attribute to Christianity the defects of such an organization. Perhaps it is necessary to explain that this is not an attack on institutional religion, which is manifestly necessary to man's spiritual welfare, even were it not quite certainly according to the mind of Christ. But even the most authentic of such institutions cannot but fail to be an inadequate incarnation of the Christian spirit, as is made obvious by the constant need of reformation which any such institution requires. The papacy itself, venerable and sacred in essence, as Catholics believe, has yet all too often betrayed Christ in action, through the worldliness, ambition or sensual weakness of those who have worn the tiara. Many wise and good men have also occupied that lofty throne; but they themselves would be the first to confess that official infallibility can co-exist with personal failure.

Yet, while we may never allow ourselves to fall into the mistake of thinking that the jewel of Christian truth can hope to find its perfect setting in this world or that the City of God is to be wholly identified with this or that particular type of policy, it is equally important to remember that the cause of Christ is not fully served by a flight from the world. Incidentally, as we have thought in the case of the Desert Fathers, such a protest may be of value; but we need to bear in mind always the simple yet profound parable in which Christ compared the kingdom of heaven with the leaven which a woman took and mixed with the flour until it was all leavened.

Such truth as there is in the accusation that Christians "sit loose to civilization"—and we have to admit that it is an accusation richly justified—is due to a failure of Christians to follow the call of their master. It is not uncommon for Christians to think of their religion as "other-worldly", which is true enough in so far, but only in so far, as we realize that this world and the values of this world are far from being the whole story. But we err if we interpret it to mean that we do not have to bother about this world and its problems. On the contrary, if there is one lesson that is central to Christ's teaching it is that the test of our sincerity as Christians is judged by certain very practical this-world tests. The priest and the Levite who did not lift a finger to help the victim of a brutal attack were condemned. They may well have muttered a prayer for the poor fellow as they carefully passed by on the other side of the road. But it was the Samaritan—who did not even belong to the right Church—who was praised, because he did something practical. The conventional exercises of piety—prayer and fasting and being meticulous about external observance—do not of themselves earn any special approbation. What does count is how we treat our fellow-men in their physical needs—hunger and thirst, poverty, homelessness and the rest.

The really shocking thing is that too many Christians have used pseudo-Christianity as a cloak for their lack of common humanity. Because they were too lazy or too selfish or too much attached to their wealth to feel impelled to come to the assistance of their needy fellow-creatures—their brothers and sisters in Christ—they soothed their consciences and attempted to justify their inaction by saying, in effect: What does it matter so long as they save their souls? And so the picture grew up of the Christian as a man who, because of a belief in the all-importance of the next life, neglected his social duty in this. It is a picture which is not wholly justified, because so many Christians—not merely the outstanding saints like Vincent de Paul, dedicated to the alleviation of poverty and disease, or Peter Claver who spent years of indescribable heroism ministering to the needs of thousands of slaves imported into America, but also countless simple folk, who cared for the sick and the unhappy in their own villages—did try to live up to the humanitarian ideals of their master. Yet enough so-called Christians have been so grossly neglectful of their common and obvious human

duty that it has all too often been left to the non-Christian
or the unbeliever to perform these tasks without any of the
inspiration which a faith in the transcendent value of every
human being ought to bring.

Worse still, this failure on the part of so many Christians
has led to the acceptance by the unbeliever of a view of the
God of the Christians which any decent and right-minded
person is bound to reject. We quoted the words of Lady
Wootton: "We no longer ask what is pleasing to God, but
what is good for man." The origins of the gross misunderstanding of the true Christian ideal which such a statement
implies spring from highly complex theological, philosophical
and ascetic considerations which we must now try to unravel.
The problem is further complicated by the fact that Christians
as a body, like the vast majority of their fellow-men, are
intellectually unsophisticated, not equipped either by natural
ability or training to appreciate the subtle nuances of doctri-
nal pronouncements, or philosophical analysis. Their pastors
(not all of whom, anyway, are richly endowed with learning
or insight), are therefore under the necessity of stating profound and subtle truths in a forthright, black-and-white sort
of way, if they are to produce any effect at all in the minds
of their listeners.

It was, incidentally, the same sort of necessity which compelled the authors of various books of the Old Testament to
clothe the great truths of creation—divine omnipotence, human disobedience, divine providence and the like—in a
series of vivid pictures and epigrammatic utterances which
have impressed themselves on the minds of believer and unbeliever alike. The intelligent believer knows that the truth
is far richer and far profounder than the pictures and the
epigrams might suggest. Unfortunately the unbeliever is able
to make fun of the simple-minded presentation, without
bothering to find out what it really implies. But the believer
does not always take the trouble to ensure that his faith is a
reasonable and adult affair, something which he can both
justify and explain to others. This reluctance is due partly

to sheer indolence but partly also to a certain nervousness or timidity which springs from a lack of genuine faith.

Indeed, it is probably fair to say that far too many Christians develop a sort of intellectual schizophrenia, keeping the truths which they hold by faith in a compartment by themselves, where they lie, perhaps for years, undisturbed by any investigation or critical appraisal. The active truths which they possess and put to use—their professional knowledge, their political ideas, their scientific attainments or technical skills—these are subject to not infrequent examination; they grow and develop, they show signs of life. But for how many Christians does their faith remain a set of formularies, slogans, consecrated phrases, which seem to bear little relation to truth as we normally understand the term. They are invested with a kind of superstitious awe, wrapped in cotton wool, put away in the attics of the mind, gathering dust, mouldering almost into decay.

It is hardly surprising then that, in face of the vigorous challenge of a crusading philosophy such as that of the modern Humanist, the believer finds himself tongue-tied and impotent. Yet St Paul insists that our worship is the worship of rational creatures[4] and St Peter exhorts us: "Be always ready with your defence when you are called to account for the hope that is in you." [5] Today, as never before, our faith calls for close argument and reasoned expression. This is not the place for religious controversy, and it is in no sectarian spirit that it is necessary to point out that Luther did a grave disservice to Christian truth when he attacked with such bitterness the philosophical basis of belief. Rejecting Aristotelian philosophy, doubtless because of its associations with the medieval Schoolmen, he will have nothing to do with the notion that "if a thing is true, it is true for philosophy and theology". Reason is only valid for the affairs of ordinary life, for earthly government ". . . that is to say, it has power to legislate and order everything regard-

[4] Rom. 12. 1.
[5] 1 Peter 3. 15.

ing this life, like drinking and eating, clothing and all that relates to external discipline and a decent life". But in things of the spirit it is not only "blind and dark"; it is "the devil's harlot. It can only blaspheme and dishonour everything that God has done." [6]

When religion becomes irrational, it inevitably finds in rationalism its greatest enemy. One thing, then, we need to do is to rediscover, if we have lost sight of it, the solid ground of reason on which our faith is established. Faith, of course, goes far beyond the reach of reason; but it in no way repudiates it, nor, indeed, can it exist in an irrational vacuum, any more than the three-dimensional cube can be itself without the plane surfaces which it yet outsoars. If Christianity were the obscurantist creed which it is sometimes made out to be, who should blame the scientist and the scholar for rejecting it? The disastrous Galileo episode is still poisoning the wells; and in modern times the unhappy debate between Bishop Wilberforce and T. H. Huxley has had lasting effects on the relations between theology and science. It is our urgent duty to make it clear to our critics that we are at one with them in the search for truth, that we are secure in the conviction that any and every kind of truth assists in the great purpose of human life, which is the discovery of God, who is revealed no less truly in the splendour and wonder of the universe than in the teaching of his own prophets. Recall the words of Coleridge: "He who begins by loving Christianity better than Truth will proceed by loving his own sect or church better than Christianity, and end by loving himself better than all."

The life of religion is not to be described in terms of cold reason, any more than the life of man can be logically analysed and scientifically categorized. Just as art and poetry, emotion and the normal exchange of civilized living clothe the stark essentials of human existence, so religion is immensely more than the acceptance by the intellect of a set of propositions coupled with a certain external regime. It is

[6] Cf. Maritain, *Three Reformers,* pp. 30-2.

the entire dedication of the whole being, body and soul, mind and heart, to the pursuit of every kind of good. Which is why, partial and incomplete as are the values which the Humanist cherishes, there can be no necessary conflict between his ideals and those of the genuine believer. Indeed, albeit without knowing it, in so far as they too worship at the shrine of truth and goodness, they are associated with us, however remotely. "As I was going round looking at the objects of your worship, I noticed among other things an altar bearing the inscription 'To an Unknown God'. What you worship but do not know—this is what I now proclaim." St Paul's words on the Areopagus have their relevance today.

But the God of the Christians is distasteful to the Humanist for reasons which are not wholly discreditable to him. Have we not made things more difficult for him by failing to realize that the portrait of the Father painted for us by the Son is bound to be more authentic than the Lord of Hosts, the jealous deity of the half-savage, warring desert nomads, fighting their way into the territories of idolatrous rivals? There are, of course, in the Old Testament, other passages of great and moving human appeal, but for far too many Christians, whose knowledge of the Old Testament is largely confined to the historical books, a grim and forbidding picture of God has come to colour their religious thinking to a deplorable extent. That picture was presented to the Jews of old presumably because it was the one best adapted to them in their stage of religious development. Far be it from me to suggest that we are all in a higher state of moral perfection than any of the Jews attained; but the fact remains that we look at life in a very different way from them; our habits of thought are altered; *we* find some of the language of, say, the Psalms, shocking, and some of the ideas ascribed to the Jewish Jehovah, to say the least, disedifying. Say, if you like, that we are more squeamish than they were: but, if we are, the language of religion needs to be suited to our temperaments if it is not to do more harm than good.

The plain truth is that all our language about God is woefully inadequate. We are trying to describe the indescribable; to suggest, therefore, that any description of God must be so complete that it never calls for qualification or interpretation is plainly untrue. St Thomas Aquinas himself remarked: *Deus melius dicitur non bonus quam bonus,* so feeble is our notion of "good" compared with the infinite perfection of the Godhead. What we need to remember and to convince ourselves of is that all human standards of justice, truth, beauty, mercy, humanity are pale reflections of, because derived from, the origin and fount of all justice, truth, beauty, mercy and humanity. That is why there can never be any sort of clash between any sort of human achievement—in itself—whether in the realm of philosophy or science, art or morality and the effortless energizing of the Being who is at once the power of thinking which lies behind all thought, the perfect harmony whence the broken chords of our earthly music derive, the radiant beauty that not the greatest artist can hope to portray.

Do we believe all this, or are we not all in danger of reducing the eternal creator to the status of a tribal God, primarily concerned with our local practices of religion but caring nothing for the splendid natural attainments of his creatures at large? As we saw in the last chapter, Sir Julian Huxley and others clearly resent and reject the whole theology of the supernatural, because it sets up an "intolerable dualism", a doctrine moreover which, as propounded, all too often seems to make a mockery of man's efforts and to suggest that it is largely a waste of time to concern oneself with the ordering of this world. Yet the whole idea of the incarnation, on which the doctrine of the supernatural depends, surely gives the lie to such a view of this world. For the incarnation can only mean that God did indeed so love the world that he came to share man's concerns, to enrich man's life in a measure far beyond its own intrinsic richness; but he did it by devoting himself to a round of activities which he shared with the craftsman, the worker, the average man.

We appreciate the wonders of the supernatural order, not

by belittling the natural order (which is after all God's handi-
work), not by encouraging men to turn their backs on their
fellow-men in order the better to serve the God who created
them, but by learning ourselves, and helping others to see,
how God has chosen to make this world of nature the vehicle
of his supernatural activity. The violin is not, of itself, capable
of producing music; equally, the violinist cannot produce
music without the violin. If it is broken or the strings are
not taut, the greatest genius will be baffled in his attempts
to produce the simplest tune. So we have to encourage ourselves to think of God, the great musician, drawing from the
instrument of our human nature the grand supernatural
strains which ring in time but echo in eternity. Rightly understood, the whole doctrine of the supernatural is not one to
inhibit our natural activity or to degrade what is called,
with some contempt, the "merely natural". Rather should
it make us more eager to develop all those natural capacities
of ours, those God-given gifts which enable us to make a
better place of this world, in the consciousness that our
earthly efforts have an abiding importance. And something
abides, even if my efforts here seem to be of no avail:

The high that proved too high; the heroic for earth too hard,
The passion that left the ground to lose itself in the sky,
Are music sent up to God by the lover and the bard:
Enough that He heard it once; we shall hear it by and by.

We must recognize that there is a theological tradition,
based on a misunderstanding of some of the more rhetorical
passages in St Augustine, propounded by Calvin and his
followers and re-asserted by the Jansenists and others, which
argues that, in consequence of the fall, human nature is
hopelessly corrupted, and that the achievement of the redemption is to substitute, as it were, for man's total failure
Christ's own achievement which, by some sort of legal fiction,
is regarded by God as our doing, even though, of course, it
is not. But the orthodox Catholic doctrine teaches that, by

the redemption, the injuries inflicted on human nature by the fall have been so healed by Christ's work that it is once again capable of action that is wholly good. The strings of the instrument have been tuned to the right pitch so that, like a violin in the hands of a master, we can produce perfect music. In the hands of the master, it is true; but the music is ours.

But this splendid and inspiring doctrine has been obscured by theological debate about the problem of grace and free-will, and since this too is an idea which the Humanist fiercely rejects, it is worthwhile looking at some misrepresentations of it to show how we have ourselves so travestied the truth that we can hardly blame any person of intelligence and sensibility for being unable to stomach what we have made of it.

This particular topic is one that has probably given rise to more theological bitterness than any other single question in the whole range of Christian teaching. In the seventeenth century in particular, Dominicans and Jesuits were practically at one another's throats, each roundly accusing the other of heresy—Dominican accusing Jesuit that the latter doctrine was indistinguishable from Pelagianism, Jesuit retorting that the other view was sheer determinism. Is it possible to suggest that they were misconceiving the nature of the problem? What seems to have bedevilled the whole debate is the notion that we have to conceive of divine grace and human volition as two distinct and to some extent opposed forces. Thus the question became a sort of mathematical one, a problem in mechanics, the human act being thought of as the resultant of two forces working at an angle to each other, so that the outcome was something that neither of the agents really wanted. Man wanted to go one way; God wanted him to go another. If God "gave" man enough grace—in other words, if he really exerted himself sufficiently—then he got his own way. But as a rule, for some obscure reason, he did not always lay on what is called "efficacious" grace. He merely gave man what is called "sufficient" grace which, in practice, never is sufficient because so often man, without going the whole hog, nevertheless ends up somewhere between what he would really like to do and what God really wants him to do.

Now this seems to me to reduce the whole of the moral life to a sort of game of chess or to one of those war-games that appear on the market from time to time. The idea that God is pushing men—and still more women, who seem peculiarly susceptible to this sort of treatment—about, throwing an extra battery of grace into the struggle at the psychological moment, means, in effect, that man is a sort of puppet. If this were remotely like the truth, who could find fault with Thomas Hardy for the attitude of mind expressed in his famous ending of *Tess of the D'Urbervilles*: "The President of the Immortals . . . had ended his sport with Tess"?

But we know that the moral struggle is a reality in which man's qualities are proved—for better or for worse. The failure is his; the achievement is his. Now, surely, we can make sense of this situation in terms of Christian theology only if we envisage grace as a power, akin to the inspiration of the artist, the enthusiasm of the idealist, the devotion of the lover. In these familiar situations, something happens to the artist, the idealist, the lover, which makes him not less but more free, not less but more himself, capable of achievements beyond the range of his "normal" personality, yet achievements which are wholly his, while brought about under the influence of this power which, coming from without, is yet accepted by him and used by him. Where the grace of God, as we say, "triumphs", the triumph is of man's making because, by his acceptance, by his co-operation, *he* has made it effective. Where grace "fails", it fails because man has refused to take advantage of it. The artist, seeing the same vision, has—for whatever reason—not been fired by it; the good man has been unable to see the quality which fired his fellow-worker to enthusiasm; and so on. Clearly all kinds of psychological, historical and other questions are here raised. But, if we are to satisfy our own minds and persuade others that our theology of grace is not a piece of fantasy bearing no relation to life as we know it, then we have to try to look at it in this sort of way.

Sir Julian Huxley and his fellow-Humanists seem to be under the impression that they are suggesting something novel when they insist that theology must start from the empirically-given, from the facts of human nature as we know them, from the findings of all the different sciences. This is no more than a restatement of a great principle of scholastic philosophy—the philosophy which provides the language in which Catholic theology is formulated: *Nihil in intellectu quod non prius fuerit in sensu*—"the doorway to the mind is through the senses". It is also, of course, the true meaning of revelation, which is simply a statement of divine truth in terms of human experience.

Obviously and supremely, it is the significance of the incarnation itself—the eternal Word of God uttered in human language, the language not merely of human speech but also of human behaviour. It is through Christ's conduct as a man, through the example he set us in the context of every-day human experience that we, his fellow-mortals, come to know what God is like.

We can in fact get at the creator only through his creation. The idea that Christians in general and Catholics in particular possess a private telephone line to God, or a closed-circuit television set on which God appears from time to time, instructing them as to what they are to believe and how they are to behave, is manifest nonsense. Yet there may well be some believers who are under the impression that this is what 'revealed religion" means. The term itself may even appear to suggest that something like this happens. But the evidence of history, in particular the history of theology, shows a very different state of things. To discover what in fact God has revealed is a matter of hard work, close reasoning, careful study of texts, linguistic and historical investigation and so on. This, incidentally, is what theologians mean when they say that theology is a science.

Take, for instance, the doctrine of the Holy Trinity—which we must clearly regard as the most refined example of a "revealed truth"—something which is certainly not discoverable by looking at those *vestigia Trinitatis,* which Augustine delighted to enumerate. How then was it discovered? Did men just dial HEAven or even DOGma, and listen to a voice dictating something like the Athanasian Creed? Not at all. If you really want to know how it came about read Fr Lebreton's *Origins of the Doctrine of the Holy Trinity.* He makes it clear how men's minds had been prepared for the acceptance of this truth almost as much by Neoplatonic speculation as by Christian analysis of the implications of certain scriptural texts.

The science of theology may not be a matter of test-tubes and reactors, thermometers, Geiger counters and the like; but it is a science which is very much tied to history and language, paleography and psychology and a host of other disciplines, as anyone who has been through a course of theology knows only too well. The idea that theologians regard themselves as people who have a special faculty for divining the divine, as water-diviners divine water, is not borne out by the evidence. Nor are they, as a body, intolerant, doctrinaire, bigoted or lacking in concern for human welfare. Just as the natural sciences progress by building on the findings of former generations—no scientist, for example, would seriously doubt the laws of electrical conduction, the law of gravity, the atomic structure of matter and so on, but does not thereby regard himself as working in blinkers, or having a closed mind—so it is unjustified to accuse the theologian of having a closed mind because he is not prepared to question certain truths which he is satisfied have been validly established.

The sad thing is, though, that some theologians—too many of them, in fact—thought that they did possess in the

Bible not merely a source-book of theological lore, but also a handbook of geology, paleontology, astronomy, biology and several other sciences, including, perhaps, political philosophy and military skill. Moreover, owing to the largely accidental fact that, during the Middle Ages, the only educated men were the clergy, it came to be thought that churchmen were not merely more intelligent and more learned than other men, but also that they knew all the answers to all possible questions. Individual theologians at times prepared to "pontificate"—it is perhaps significant that the term came to be employed in this sense—on matters on which the pope himself might hesitate to express an opinion.

All that is changed. The spread of education, the separation of theological discipline from most other subjects, the astonishing rise of the natural sciences to their present position of eminence, have meant that matters which were once regarded as somehow akin to religion are allowed to exist, so to say, in their own right. This has been, in some ways, of great benefit to both sides. And although it looks as though "religion" has withdrawn from interfering in certain fields, the essential rôle of religion is not altered. It may well have been purified by being allowed, indeed encouraged, to concentrate its attention on what alone matters to it.

One can therefore understand how Lady Wootton could speak as she did in the passage quoted above. Nor, clearly, is she very much to blame for not reading between the lines of history. But I hope that what has been said in the course of this chapter will enable us to see that there is no essential conflict between any kind of truth and the truths of faith; that far from being nervous of scientific discovery, we should welcome any contribution that anyone can make, to help us to understand the world of God's making, so that we may descry a little more clearly the lineaments of his own visage; that we should confess our shortcomings in all this matter, and realize that we have been a cause of scandal to our scientific friends, because we have presented the truth, in our lives, as something which was not really related to any other sort of truth—almost as if there were two sets of values, two standards of reality. In particular, perhaps, we have failed to appreciate adequately the relations between the natural and the supernatural.

CHAPTER III

THE INADEQUACIES
OF HUMANISM

We said in a previous chapter that the modern system of thought which goes by the name of Humanism is not an essentially novel phenomenon. The label "evolutionary" which Sir Julian Huxley has attached to this latest manifestation of a perennial attitude of mind is no more significant than is the colouring matter which the pharmaceutical chemist puts into his specifics. It is very much "the mixture as before". We shall now try to analyse this recurrent tendency in man's thinking, taking account of any special elements which may be found in the contemporary brand. We shall then see why, apart altogether from the data of Christian revelation, this system is both inadequate and self-contradictory.

Fundamentally, the Humanist would hold that not merely is it unnecessary to look beyond man for the key to the riddle of the universe, it is in fact impossible. On the face of it, this seems an entirely reasonable proposition. After all, in our experience, all knowledge, all thinking begin with man. In the famous words of Protagoras: "Man is the measure of everything." And our experience *must* be the final court of appeal. For the very imagining of, the mere speculation about, the existence of beings higher than ourselves is still part of our experience. Our eyes, our ears bring us reports of events beyond ourselves; our telescopes bring us information about worlds beyond our world, systems beyond our solar system; but these things exist for us only in so far as we get these reports of them. Who is to say what they

are really like "in themselves"? Would they have any meaning
at all if that meaning were not conferred on them by the
processes of our minds? How loud is a gramophone in the
desert, with no one to hear it?

And so the whole positivist philosophy developed, the
doctrine that all meaning is imposed on the world by men,
that nothing at all has any significance or any value except
in so far as these are attributed by man. Parallel with this
doctrine is the whole secularist outlook, the rejection of
any world, any order of reality, other than that which falls
under man's immediate gaze. So God is rejected, and immortality. The ground is cut from under the feet of the
man who maintains that, over and above the world of our
immediate sense-experience, there is a world of richer significance, or more abiding importance, of greater reality.

What are we to say about all this?

Well, first of all let us suppose that what the positivist says
is in fact true. We are then faced with the remarkable situation that all man's greatest and most inspiring ideals are
completely bogus. Man, whose whole experience of life
ought to convince him that his brief and shabby story ends
with the grave; that all he can do is to hand something on to
the next generation, which, in turn improving on what he has
done, will hand it on to the next, until finally this planet
freezes to death and the whole story will come to an end
and nobody will be there to record it or to remember it:
man yet remains obstinately convinced that that is not the
way things are.

> Hope springs eternal in the human breast;
> Man never is, but always to be blest;
> The soul, uneasy and confined from home,
> Rests and expatiates in a life to come.

Poor fool living in his unsubstantial paradise of his own
creating!

But the odd thing is that he is *capable* of such a creation.
If it be true that

We are such stuff
as dreams are made on, and our little life
Is rounded with a sleep

how could we possibly have come to think otherwise?

It is all put down to wishful thinking. We are like children, weaving lovely fantasies to comfort ourselves in the dark, whistling to keep our spirits up. But, if we look at this allegation critically, we shall see that it is not an argument at all. The child is capable of weaving fantasies precisely because there *is* a whole world of reality beyond his little bedroom. He has accumulated a store of knowledge which enables him to picture to himself a set of comforting visions, because—whether these particular visions are *like* objective reality or not—even the mind of a child is not limited to the here and now, but can reach out beyond his present experiences to something other than himself and his own emotions, to rest in the thought of a fairyland of romance, where everybody is beautiful and kind, and he himself is a great prince, with a lovely princess and all the rest of it. What the positivist asks us to believe is that there is nothing but the bedroom, to which the child's experience is limited. It is this great leap of the mind, from the limited experience of the here and now to the conception of an order of things of which this world is a function, which the positivist does not, indeed cannot, justify.

Doubtless he will seize on the word "function" and say, roundly: "Precisely. Man's reasoning capacity is such that he can generalize from particular instances, he can construct mathematical and other systems, reaching beyond the particular instance, which is seen as a specimen of larger class." "Clearly," he will say, "I do not deny that the mind has this remarkable creative gift. The evidence for that is obvious. What I refuse to admit is that there is any evidence for the gigantic construction which you people put on it, building a vast scheme of things, including a God who, on your own admission, is utterly unlike anything on earth, postulating an immortality which is clean contrary to such evidence as we do possess, and, in general, refusing to allow your thinking to be controlled by the only possible test—that of experimental verification or, at least, of induction from the facts of experience."

But, of course, there are many things which the most hardened positivist accepts, which are incapable of that sort of treatment. To begin with, he has no sort of test or proof by which he can convince himself or others that his is not the only intelligence in an otherwise mindless world. The logic of the positivist, who will accept as true nothing that he cannot test by some sort of submission to experience, would if pursued logically lead to solipsism, that terrible condition so vividly portrayed by Chesterton, in which a man

> doubts not the existence of angels, but the existence of men and cows. For him his own friends are a mythology made up by himself. He created his own father and his own mother. This horrible fancy has in it something decidedly attractive to the somewhat mystical egoism of our own day. . . . When all this kindly world all round the man has blackened out like a lie; when friends fade into ghosts, and the foundations of the world fail; then, when the man believes in nothing and in no man, is alone in his own nightmare, then the great individualistic motto shall be written over him in avenging irony. The stars will be only dots in the blackness of his own brain; his mother's face will be only a sketch from his own insane pencil on the walls of his cell. But over his cell shall be written, with dreadful truth, "He believes in himself".

In other words, sanity itself is based not on logic or experiment but on an act of faith, not, of course, an act of faith in the theological sense but in the sense that there are a number of ideas or principles in which men believe, anterior to logic and experiment, because they are the very ground and basis of all possible experiment or debate. Unless we accept the axiom that all human minds work in approximately the same way—an axiom which entails the notion that there are existent realities which for convenience we label human minds; the further axiom that, in the same conditions, objects behave in the same way; the further axiom that there are certain laws of thought which are anterior to all convention, and indeed make convention possible: unless we do this, we shall never get anywhere at all.

The whole argument that lies behind the modern evolutionary theory, the very argument which made it possible for Charles Darwin to correlate certain observed phenomena and produce the *Origin of Species,* demands a framework within which it was possible for what is described as evolution to take place, apart altogether from the possibility of its being studied. That is to say, whether or no we attribute to natural processes anything in the nature of purpose, we must at least start by accepting something to be loosely described as *tendency.* If we accept, as a purely scientific description of certain events—and there is no difficulty in accepting it in principle—the picture drawn by the thorough-going evolutionist, we get something like this: We must postulate the existence of a primitive state of affairs in which all that existed was a mass, in the form, presumably, of an immensely dense atomic body which, in virtue of its interior stresses, expanded, exploded, developed, disintegrated, always in such a way as to produce those atomic groupings which provide the fabric of the universe. For perhaps two and a half billion years this process has continued, until today we are presented with a universe, still expanding, into regions beyond the range of the most powerful radio telescope, the only radio telescopes we know of being situated on what is, in the scale of the totality of things, a trivial speck of matter which has become the home of a type of being possibly unique in the whole cosmos. From the earliest ages the process has gone on, until what started as intensely powerful yet essentially inanimate matter has produced the architecture of the Parthenon, the plays of Shakespeare, the music of Beethoven, the moral teaching of Confucius, the glory of daffodils

That come before the swallow dares and take
The winds of March with beauty

and so on, without end.

On any theory, it is an awe-inspiring story. For the moment, we must disregard the religious explanation, and look at that given by the evolutionary Humanist. According to him, nothing of all this was "meant". It just happened that way. Since we human beings are the end-product of the process, we are inclined to flatter ourselves that it was all, in the strict sense, for our benefit. But we must be careful. The fact that it has all turned out so much for our benefit—although we have a long way to go until we have directed the rest of the story to our entire satisfaction (for now, as we all know, man has become capable of controlling what was hitherto uncontrolled)—this fact must not lead us into boasting that, two and a half billion years ago, there was any intention that it should work out this way. Any purpose we may descry in this tremendous energizing is a subjective attribution of some controlling power for whose presence there is no sort of evidence at all.

And yet, the odd thing is that on any scale short of the cosmic we do not merely attribute purpose; we both demand it and discover it. We spend much of our time making sure that things work out in a certain way. We feel baffled and frustrated if we are unable to find an explanation for an ordinary event. If I am driving a car and become conscious of a curious ticking noise, I am unhappy until I have located it and found an explanation for it. We see the whole of our experience as conditioned by a whole chain of causal connections. If we want to launch a capsule to the moon, we study the laws of mechanics in the minutest detail, because we know that this is how the motion of material bodies is controlled. If we spend hundreds of millions of dollars on putting a man into orbit, we do not just say: "Oh, well, of course, the whole thing is pretty chancy, but there *is* a chance in a million that this thing will come off." On the contrary, if we were not absolutely convinced that throughout the universe still marched "the army of unalterable law" we should not be tempted to waste our money.

Now the puzzling thing is why so many scientists, dedicated as they are to the proposition that any event within the universe has an explanation which more often than not can be discovered, are yet unwilling to follow their conviction out to its logical conclusion and demand an explanation for the whole thing. While they maintain that, like Topsy, the universe just "growed" and while they can, to some extent, explain the process, they seem satisfied to accept the view that no explanation is called for to account for this remarkable state of affairs—the actual existence of a universe so marvellously rich and fertile. Even were the initial state of affairs simply that of an inert mass, which never developed at all, even that would call for some explanation. If a housewife finds a lump of soil on the drawing-room carpet, she doesn't just shrug her shoulders and say: "Oh, well, that's the way things are." She says, in a stern voice: "Who didn't wipe his feet on the mat?" She knows the mud is there because somebody brought it there. But the sceptical scientist does not seem to find it at all odd that we can start with a situation which is much more astonishing than the presence of a bit of mud on the carpet. For we start with a situation which, somehow, contains within itself the total explanation of all the stupendous things that have happened since. In the words of Horace: *Credat Judaeus Apella: non ego.*

Most of us, at one time or another, have asked the question: "Why should there be anything at all?" Perhaps this is hopelessly naïve. Certainly the scientific Humanist never seems to allow himself to put the same question, which in many ways would seem to be the most fundamental question of all, on the Humanist's own principles. For he insists, again and again, that we must start with our own experience and follow where the argument leads. Now, the argument has led him to the point where he becomes illogical, where he deserts his own principles, where he becomes irrational and unscientific. For he here abandons that causal chain of interconnected phenomena which has brought him to this point.

The fact is that the Humanist, for all his boasting, is not genuinely open-minded, He accuses the believer of having a closed mind, of being forbidden to think freely for himself; but, in comparison with the tenacious dogmatism of the Humanist who declares that there cannot be anything beyond this world of space and time, even the most reactionary of fundamentalists is remarkably open-minded. It really is time this particular misrepresentation of the facts were shown up clearly for what it is. Rowland Hill, as we know, "did not see why the devil should have all the good tunes". We do not see, either, why the title to be rational, open-minded and honest should be denied to the believer merely because he is not prepared to surrender certain truths which he believes to have been established at least as surely as the truths of science.

For, in asserting that there must be an order of reality beyond this space-time world, we are only taking the argument of scientific reasoning one step further—an important and highly significant step, it is true, and one which takes us into regions about which the processes of the physical sciences can tell us nothing. But to say that we are thereby somehow shutting our eyes to the facts is a curious *non sequitur*. One of the most misleading of such accusations was contained in an article which Sir Julian Huxley published in the *Observer* (July 17th, 1960), in which occurs the following remarkable passage:

> Christian theology has a highly organized theoretical structure, based on a combination of an elaborate god-theory with a subsidiary but equally elaborate soul-theory. It can develop only within certain limits: the fixed postulates of its basic god-theory set limits to its range of applicability, while its reliance on the authority of divine intervention and revelation limits its powers of self-correction. Humanism, on the other hand, is acquiring a well-organized theoretical basis in the form of a comprehensive theory of evolution as a whole. It is an open system, capable of unlimited develop-

ment; its only postulate is a thoroughgoing naturalism, so that all phenomena are grist to its mill. Its reliance on scientific method makes it automatically self-correcting.

How noble and splendid it all sounds. But, of course, it would be child's play to rewrite the passage in precisely the opposite sense, to be rude about the limitations of Humanism, as Sir Julian is rude about Christian theology, and to wax eloquent about the limitless prospects before the latter. Only, rudeness and rhetoric are rarely combined with reasoned discussion. If we are to arrive at that mutual understanding which is desirable on practical as well as theoretical grounds, we must try to maintain the courtesies of civilized debate.

Now, whatever may have been true of some past ages, it is most emphatically not true today to assert that the theologian uses any sort of *a priori* deduction from information handed out to him from some heavenly information centre to obviate the necessity for reasoned analysis of the content of his faith. On the contrary, the theologian is beholden to the scientific worker in various fields for the help they afford him in his own field. The theologian is only too eager to learn from the scientist, and that not merely as an intelligent observer of the cosmic scene but also precisely as a theologian. Believing as he does that any advance in human knowledge is bound to shed light on the great problem of human existence and human destiny, he does his best, often with much labour, to try to keep up with scientific progress. If, then, it is true that Humanism's "reliance on scientific method makes it automatically self-correcting", this means that theology too is automatically self-correcting. Only, just as the philosopher and the scientist know that there are certain basic truths in their fields which no sort of discovery is going to disprove, so too does the theologian.

Suppose, for example, that some physicist were to find that, as a result of an experiment, it looked as though the law of gravity was, in fact, a myth, what would his reaction be? Surely, he would go over his calculations very carefully indeed, to see where he had gone wrong. He would not take it for granted at the outset that his experiment had disproved the law of gravity. No one would therefore say that he was not keeping his mind open to the possibility that the law of gravity might turn out after all to be a kind of universal delusion. To have certain clear principles in mind is not to have a closed mind, for the mind can only operate on the basis of some accepted system. How is it possible to assert that one has a perfectly open mind and to say, at the same time, that any form of supernatural view of reality is excluded? This is not openness of mind; it is simple prejudice. What would a man like Sir Julian Huxley say to someone who began a treatise on modern science by asserting that, of course, he was not prepared to consider the possibility that evolution or, shall we say, Einstein's theory of relativity might be true. Yet this is precisely the attitude of mind revealed in the assertion that Humanism's "only postulate is a thorough-going naturalism".

Doubtless, one major reason why the Humanist today takes up this anti-supernaturalist position may well spring from the failures of too many believers to appreciate the significance of their own faith, not least in its application to the problems of this world. We honour and rightly honour the Humanist for his concern with the needs of humanity, for the patient labour which he devotes to the alleviation of distress, to the amelioration of the human lot; where we should like to join issue with him is over the idea that the religions of mankind in general, and the Christian religion in particular, are essentially opposed to the ideals of his system of thought. May we refer again to a sentence from a passage by Sir Julian Huxley which was quoted above? The unified framework of ideas which he calls Evolutionary Humanism, he says "assigned man to his proper place in nature, and showed him his true destiny".

Man's proper place in nature, as the modern evolutionist sees it, is to be the chief, if not the sole, agent for the future evolution of this planet. This clearly implies that evolution in the future, whatever it may have been in the past, is to be purposive, directed by intelligence, with some definite goal in view. It is perhaps a little unkind of us to remark that we can see no reason for refusing to evolution, as it has been in the past, that purposive quality which it is now to assume for the future. Hitherto, apparently, the process of evolution has been purely mechanical, working through blind chance, though controlled by some sort of law—the law of natural selection. If we are to try to understand what this means, it looks as if we shall have to accept the idea that, for no assignable reason, the nature of things is such that, out of a formless chaos arose the astonishing variety of chemical elements, biological types, intellectual attainments, which is the world as we know it. Or is it perhaps truer to claim that the observer of these processes discovers a purposive activity, if not in the overall pattern at least in the behaviour of individual animals? The law of natural selection works through the instinctive avoidance by the swifter antelope of perils which destroy his slower cousins.

Once again, if there is purpose in the individual event, why should we deny purpose to the whole cosmic process? This can only be because the Humanist is not prepared to accept the implications of such a notion. One suspects that, like the ostrich, he is burying his head in the arid sand of his own preconceptions. (Incidentally, if it is true that ostriches do behave in this curious way, how on earth did they come to survive?) The simple truth seems to be that the best argument against a purposeless process of natural selection is Charles Darwin himself, described by von Hugel as "obsessed by outlooks immensely beyond all empirical observation". If there is no purpose in evolution, it is difficult to see how there can be any sort of pattern. Yet, in fact, it is the sheerest perversity to try to maintain that what is *later* is regarded by us as better only in virtue of some standard which we have invented ourselves and imposed on what has happened. The pattern which Darwin saw in nature was not invented and imposed by him; it was discovered by him, imposed on his mind by its very obvious presence "out there".

It is surely to be obsessed by an attitude of mind clean contrary to all normal experience to seek to maintain that it was sheer chance that brought Socrates and Gandhi, Virgil and da Vinci, Michelangelo and Malcolm Sargent out of a fortuitous collection of stuff that happened to be lying about. This is clean contrary to all our experience; it is only by refusing to recognize that he is abandoning the famous scientific principle of sitting down before the facts like a little child, that the evolutionary Humanist can go on maintaining his position. For there is absolutely nothing in our experience which can justify the attitude of mind which believes that, by some intrinsic mechanism, an inferior type of being can produce a superior one.

The Humanist may perhaps point to the fact that what we call precious stones are produced from ordinary chemicals fused together under great heat and great pressure. But, of course, it is only by a man-made convention that diamonds are regarded as more valuable than simple carbons and the like. If I were cast away on a desert island, I should not regard myself as particularly fortunate if I discovered that it was littered with diamonds, but that there was absolutely nothing to eat. I would gladly swap a diamond necklace for a string of sausages. . . .

A problem is certainly raised by recent experiments which, at first sight, seem to have produced living matter out of the juxtaposition of non-living chemical elements. But before we regard this as the exception proving our general rule, we should have to be satisfied on one or two points; either that the chemical elements so compounded did not somehow contain seeds of life, sparked off, as it were, by their very juxtaposition or, alternatively, that the resulting compound was genuinely living, that is possessing some new intrinsic principle in virtue of which it could now operate in ways characteristic of living things, and was not an essentially mechanical contrivance, capable of producing effects that simulate life, rather like the amputated frog's leg, galvanized into activity by the application of an electric current.

This may sound very much like special pleading. The argument is simply that this seems a case for applying Hume's well-known objection to miracles—that the whole of our experience is so entirely opposed to such happenings that we cannot really be expected to believe them. The entertaining thing is, incidentally, that men who would readily reject the very possibility of miracles on Humian principles are more than ready to accept a whole picture of reality—I mean the thoroughgoing doctrine of evolution—with no sort of empirical evidence to support it. Let us repeat, for the sake of clarity, that we do not reject the evolutionary theory as a description of what may well have taken place: what is difficult to understand is the idea that it all took place through sheer, uncontrolled, blind, purposeless struggle.

What we may claim, then, is that the man who, for whatever reason, is not prepared to accept the thoroughgoing doctrine described by Sir Julian as "the slow biological improvement effected by the blind opportunistic workings of natural selection" is being truer to the spirit of scientific enquiry than is the man who accepts such a view. It is true that Sir Julian himself seems, at times, to want to have it both ways. Natural selection, he says elsewhere (*Observer,* July 17th, 1960) ". . . far from being a matter of chance as is often unthinkingly asserted, is an orderly process. As Darwin himself pointed out, it inevitably leads to the improvement of organisms in relation to the conditions of life. It is an automatic regulating and directive agency. . . ." Yet, almost immediately he goes on to say: "Adaptation is no proof of conscious design. The same holds for the gradual evolution of high types with immensely enlarged capacities. . . ."

To quote the author himself, in the same article, this time with reference to a theological statement of Dr Mascall's: "This, I must confess, seems to me mere double-talk." What is this adaptation which is the outcome of "blind opportunistic workings", but which "far from being a matter of chance . . . is an orderly process"? Can you have a "regulative and directive agency" which is in no way intelligent or controlled by intelligence?

No, on the whole, it looks very much as if—despite all the difficulties inherent in the theistic position (difficulties about which we shall have something to say in the next chapter)— reason and logic are more on the side of the believer than in favour of the Humanist.

But it is high time to turn to another important reason why, again on the Humanist's own principles, we find his position so unsatisfactory. It is, as we know, in the sacred name of humanity that he rejects any transcendental ideas—God, as a reality distinct from, yet somehow controlling this world; God, as the ultimate source of all truth, which is fragmentarily revealed to man in various ways; God, as the source and origin of the moral law; God, as the giver of life, in this world as in the next.

The chief reason why such ideas are repugnant to the Humanist—leaving out of account now those perversions of them which have sprung from our misrepresentation of them —is that they appear to diminish the dignity of man, to destroy the reality of his power as a free agent, to distract him from the real purpose of existence, which is to bring about on this earth a paradise in which peace and justice will prevail and men will be at leisure to enjoy the good life of artistic enjoyment, physical satisfaction, emotional and intellectual fulfilment. (Regrettably, perhaps, one is so reminded of Sydney Smith's idea of heaven—"eating *pâté de foie gras* to the sound of trumpets. . . .")

First of all, without introducing the notion of a personal God, let us recognize that man is not, in fact, the lord of creation, making and unmaking natural laws to his liking, modifying objective truth to pleas himself. As Bossuet remarked: "The greatest intellectual failing is that of believing in things because we should like them to be so and not because we have seen that they are so in fact." One of the extraordinary fallacies of the Humanist position is that its supporters seem to imagine that, if only they can free man from the thraldom of believing in God, they will somehow have rendered him supremely free to go his own way. But, of course, whether God exists or not—assuming for the moment that we can think him away—man will not be in any way enriched; he will be terribly impoverished. He will still be bound by the great scheme of truth, to which, if he is to progress at all, he must wholeheartedly submit himself. The great principles upon which all man's right thinking depend will remain immovably established, eternal as the deity we have rejected, immutable as the heaven we have cast away. Whether or not truth is, as the believer holds, one face of God, man must submit himself to it if he is to prosper.

So it is with the great laws that control man's conduct— whether we think of the laws that govern the operation of the forces of nature or the law of man's being to which he must submit if he is to be himself. Abolish God, if you can, we may say to the Humanist; but what practical good is it going to do you? Will you take out of human experience the heartbreak and loneliness, the pain and the terror, the misery and degradation? The Humanist finds, in the existence of evil, what he regards as a paramount argument against the existence of God. But at least the Christian holds that God cares about evil and suffering, that he has shared man's sorrows, that he has turned suffering into its own antidote.

Again, the Humanist seems to imagine that, by getting rid of God, he will somehow make the moral law at once more effective and less onerous. While we may wholeheartedly agree with him that the perfection of moral conduct consists in doing the right because it is right and not out of fear of punishment or hope of reward, it is difficult to see why it is not both more human and more inspiring to see that law not as some blind, impersonal scheme but as the manifestation of a loving purpose for man's own great benefit. One of the great messages of the Christian faith is that the whole law is summed up in love—love not alone of one's fellowmen, but of the wise power guiding man to his greater happiness.

Which brings us to our final point. The great failure of the Humanist creed is that it casts away the whole basis on which its own ideals can find any support. It is intellectually bewildering to reflect that an age which has become increasingly secular in outlook pays increasing homage to the ideal of democracy. For on any purely phenomenological view what possible justification can one find for any belief in the essential equality of all men? Look round any casual collection of human beings, and the thing that is most striking is how utterly unequal they are—unequal in talent and character, unequal in physical endowment, social ranking, political outlook, and so on throughout the whole catalogue of human characteristics. We may respect and admire the often passionate concern of the Humanist for his suffering fellow-men in distant corners of the world. But if man is, in essence, one with the beasts that perish, why should we so bitterly resent and so vigorously condemn the barbarities practised on Jew or African, Algerian or Armenian, Huguenot or Catholic. It is all a part of that evolutionary process, which has, in the past, thrown up *Homo Sapiens* and is now, apparently, on the way to producing a race of *Sapientiores,* the Humanists.

But if, as the Humanist explicitly does, you reject all absolutes, how can you blame men for not accepting your particular type of fastidiousness? It is all, in the end, a matter of taste.

But we know it is not, and by "we" is meant not merely the Christian who believes that all men are made in the image of God, that in Christ there is "neither Jew nor Gentile, bond nor free"; we mean the Humanist too, whose heart is so much more in the right place than is his head. Implicitly, unconsciously, even against his conscious philosophy he stands with us in this faith in the supreme importance of the human spirit. Sir Julian Huxley may pour scorn on what he terms the "soul-hypothesis" of the Christian's theology. It is not necessary to quarrel with him about words. For, unless he believes in something like what we call the soul, he cannot possibly justify or defend his basic humanitarian attitudes, unless he falls back on an appeal to emotion—a strange refuge for a rationalist.

In his chapter entitled "The Democratic Challenge", Francis Williams speaks as follows:

> The history of political advance is the history of ever-widening loyalties. The loyalties we now require have to be wide enough to embrace the continuing human race as a whole, even though they still contain within themselves smaller and earlier loyalties which have their own validity in their own context. Humanism offers the possibility of such a loyalty. It sees man in his true stature as the highest product and only agent of the evolutionary process, called upon by his destiny constantly to explore and extend the frontiers of knowledge so that he may better understand his own nature and the environment in which he lives. . . . It is not, of course, possible to promise that, by the light of humanism, we shall progress unhampered to greater political understanding. Men although rational are not wholly or always so . . . but at least Humanism builds no deliberate barriers to human understanding and sets no booby-traps of its own along the political road. Nor does it ask that those who travel shall be blindfolded. It makes instead the revolutionary proposal that we should advance with our eyes open and our minds ready to learn from experience. . . .

To which, of course, anybody, Christian or not, is bound to say *Amen*. But it is not limpidly obvious what precisely Humanism is offering in the concrete situation. If I am invited to contribute to a fund for relieving distress in the Congo, am I really going to be inspired by the thought that those starving children are "the highest product and only agent of the evolutionary process"? If a tramp asks me for the price of a drink, shall I reflect: "Here is a man called upon by his destiny constantly to explore and extend the frontiers of knowledge"? You know, if that sort of thing were pronounced from the pulpit, it is probable that the reactions of many in the congregation would be: "Claptrap!" Is it really an improvement on the age-old appeal: "As long as you did it to the least of these my little ones, you did it to me"?

This is not mocking the Humanist. In many ways he is

admirable, and much of his zeal and enthusiasm may well put us Christians to shame. What we are saying is that he is much better than his philosophy might suggest. The Christian view of life, however much it may have been betrayed by its representatives, yet remains the noblest statement of human values that the world has ever seen. Even the pagan Aristotle saw that Humanism was not enough: "Nor should we heed those who bid us remember that we are but men and should think only what is at the human level, that we are but mortal and should think but mortal thoughts: no, as far as in us lies, let us put on immortality. . . ."

How the Humanist ideal—and so much else—finds its fulfilment in Christianity will be discussed in the next chapter. In the meantime, we may recall Chesterton's words

It is only Christian men
Guard even pagan things.

CHAPTER IV

INTEGRAL CHRISTIANITY

At the outset of this discussion, it was stated that an examination of two systems of thought—that of the Humanist and that of the Christian—would show that, far from being mutually hostile, the two are substantially in agreement, that each needs the other to complement it, or rather that Christianity includes whatever is of value in Humanism. We are now in a position to see how far this claim can be justified. What I should like to do in the first part of this final section is to sketch out what I believe to be the basic Christian position, without argument, without any attempt to justify it or to defend it, but simply to state it in such a way that the Humanist should be able to see whether or not such an ideal is in any vital way at variance with his own convictions. We may then have an opportunity to discuss a little more fully, to explain and to defend some of the puzzles which the unbeliever not unnaturally finds in the Christian's outlook.

For the Christian, then, the central fact, the abiding truth is the perfection of wisdom and love, not in the fragmentary and imperfect form in which we human beings experience it, but realized and achieved in the life of the Godhead. For he sees God not as a tepid, remote and rather boring entity, but as a society of three immensely, nay infinitely rich, indescribably active and vital persons. A fundamental aspect of the life of the Godhead is the selfless love which issues in that creative act which called into existence this astonishing universe, with its mixture of beauty and goodness and truth. Wherever we encounter things that are beautiful, activities that are good, truths of whatever sort, we recognize that we are in the presence of something elemental, something of abiding significance. The butterfly that brightens a summer day exists briefly and perishes: but the glimpse of beauty which it has brought to us is, as we well know, a manifestation of something which does not perish, even though it be withdrawn from our sight. The heroic or generous act, which may cost the life of him who performs it, has about it a timeless quality which endures. The scientist or the scholar who makes a new discovery is not creating truth; he is discovering something already there. And all this notion, far from diminishing the value of our human experiences, gives them surely an added importance, a worthwhileness quite beyond the scope of what is merely transitory and perishable.

But, as we all know, this world of our experience is not a wholly delightful one. Side by side with the joy and the beauty goes much that is imperfect and disturbing. The traditional theological term used to express this state of affairs is Original Sin, a term which, unfortunately, has become so involved in theological debate that it is in serious danger of being divorced from reality as we know it. While it is true that all that is depends, in the last resort, upon the creative *fiat* of God, it is equally true that that same act has given to its offspring an individuality of their own, so that they are distinct from their maker and in some mysterious way stand on their own feet. Yet because they are not God, because they are finite, limited and therefore inadequate manifestations of the Being who gave them being, they are incapable, of themselves, of doing anything but restrict and in some sense resist the divine action.

The charming, naïve, yet at the same time profoundly meaningful story of the fall of man symbolizes this state of affairs in a way that is so striking that it has entered into all Christian thinking and has had an influence far beyond the bounds of both Judaism and Christianity. For it describes vividly and precisely that strange tension within human beings—on the one hand the need for law, for submission to authority and, on the other, the desire to be free, to be independent, to make trial of experiences which will give us knowledge of good and evil. Seeking what we believe to be desirable and, in that sense, good, we come to know and to do evil. Striving to be more than we are, we discover our essential inadequacy, our helplessness, our nakedness. In St Augustine's searing aphorism: *Nemo habet de suo nisi mendacium atque peccatum.* "Left to himself, all that man achieves is lying and wickedness." It is really the point of Rousseau's dictum: "Man is born free and is everywhere in chains." He has destroyed his own freedom; he has forged his own fetters. Both are rhetorical exaggerations; but both testify to a profound truth.

This is, of course, all very shocking and distasteful to the Humanist with his simple faith in the natural perfectibility of human nature. But the sad truth is that all man's achievements contain within themselves the seeds of their own frustration. Again and again, throughout the history of mankind, inventions fraught with promise have turned out to be charged with menace. The latest and most apocalyptic manifestation of this truth is to be found, of course, in man's development of the tremendous power derived from nuclear fission, a discovery which puts at his disposal a source of energy which may improve the conditions of his life to a degree almost unimaginable; but a power which may equally well destroy the cultural inheritance of five thousand years. This is an obvious truth which not all the wishful thinking and nebulous optimism of those who believe in the immaculate conception of all human beings can falsify.

Fortunately for him, man has not been left entirely to his own dubious devices. Over and above the capacities and abilities which man possesses "in his own right", the Christian doctrine of the supernatural declares that God has put at man's disposal a further deeper power, a mysterious elevation of his nature until its inherent defects and limitations are transcended in a sharing of God's own life and power. It is this truth which lies at the basis of the doctrine of the incarnation. For, by becoming man, by sharing in man's way of life without losing his essential Godhead, Christ has caught up our human activities into the very experience of the Godhead itself.

Yet this remarkable event inevitably raises some of the greatest puzzles and paradoxes of the Christian faith. For, in becoming man, Christ necessarily confined himself to one particular human sphere, involved himself in one specific human situation. Born of a Jewish mother in the days of Herod the king, he was caught up in that tangled and complex religious and political world which was the world of Judaism in the last decades of its existence as an independent, recognizable national unit. Not only, for example, was the individual quality of his social background, with all that that meant of manners of behaving, forms of thought and speech, style of living and so forth, uniquely his, in a way which cannot be shared by the vast majority of his followers, but the very process of our redemption through his life-giving death has been irrevocably related to a manner of execution—crucifixion—which has stamped on Christian worship and much Christian devotion a character which might seem almost inescapably to remove it from real life (and indeed real death) as we experience it.

All this has meant that Christianity has about it a flavour of the remote past, of a world that is gone. Unless we are careful, it almost becomes a study in archaeology. The responsibility of the Christian is to make sure that this does not happen, that, while our religion is necessarily linked with and indeed based on a memory of the past, it is equally to be seen as very much of today and tomorrow. The fact that God became man at a given moment in time invests that moment with a central significance which is aptly symbolized by our method of dating all other events in the world's history according to the calendar of Christ's nativity. But it is not fidelity to, it is betrayal of, the very meaning and purpose of the incarnation if we do not see the continuing development of man's thought and achievement as an extension of the incarnation, in that it is an extension of man himself. For while

Christ was that individual man and no other, while the outward shape and pattern of his life was, in so many ways, as we have said, so different from ours, yet it is basically one with ours, in that it is a genuine human life, marked by all these characteristics of intellectual growth, humane sympathy and moral fulfilment which are of the essence of a true humanity.

Take, for example, the astonishing broadening of man's world-picture which has taken place over the last nineteen hundred years and, especially, over the last century and a half. Because Christ, in his normal human consciousness, was concerned with a world that was limited in outlook to the Mediterranean basin, knowing nothing of the wide-ranging astronomical vision which we today take entirely for granted; because his eyes never looked on any but the most primitive features of life (as we think of them), knowing nothing of the motor-car, the steam-engine, the aeroplane, radio, television, gas and electricity and atomic energy, we tend to think of these every-day things as not merely not related to Christianity but as positively incapable of being thought of in Christian terms. It is probably this psychological fact more than any other which is responsible for the unease, the tension which we feel to exist between the modern world and our religion.

But if Christ worked at the carpenter's bench with a few simple tools, knowing nothing of circular saws and electric drills, still less of the conveyor belt and the vast machines of our industrialized society, the difference is relatively superficial and insignificant. For Jesus of Nazareth remains absolutely one with the craftsman, the industrial worker, the artisan—one with them in the possession of trained hand and eye, one in the sense of effort rewarded, in the control by man of his material, in the service of his fellow-man which is the common lot of mankind.

This is the abiding truth and the abiding significance of the incarnate experience of the God-man, an experience which we all share, in which we are made one with him. For only so shall we understand the broad human realities of our faith, which, seen aright, are the common ground for the Humanist and for us, who believe in a world of value transcending yet not denying all the greatness and glory of man's ambitions and man's achievements.

Sir Julian Huxley somewhere quotes the famous line of the Roman poet Terence to express the ideal of the Humanist— *Homo sum: humani nil a me alienum puto.* "Man that I am, I exclude from my purview nothing of all that belongs to man." But, of course, these words express equally truly the outlook of Christ, as they should express the outlook of every genuine Christian. Christ's healing touch and sympathetic word were at the disposal of all, whatever their need, their social condition, their race. The Roman centurion profited no less than the ruler of the synagogue; the sinful woman was made his friend as well as the tax-gatherer and the fisherman. The housewife and the farmer, the rich employer and the monarch, the wine-merchant and the architect provided him with subjects for his preaching and his parables. Incredible as it may well seem to many a Humanist, he is the first and greatest of all Humanists.

Moreover, just as when we were thinking of creation we insisted that God's creatures were not God's puppets but were given by their creator an independent reality of their own, so the incarnation does not mean that the whole responsibility for man's supernatural well-being is taken out of his hands. On the contrary, one very important aspect of this doctrine is that it means that man's redemption is achieved from within mankind, and through the natural activities of man. What not only the Humanists but far too many Christians fail to realize is that the genuine relationship between man and God, at the natural and supernatural levels, is that man is made not so much to be God's slave as to be his partner. In all his manifold works, man is as it were developing the resources which creation contains, promoting his own welfare by using aright and according to their own natures the manifold riches contained in God's world, which is also man's world. This, incidentally, is why we can gladly welcome the thesis of the modern Humanist that man's function is to control the further course of the evolutionary process. For this is clearly what is meant by man's duty to serve God. That service is performed best precisely through the operation of man's faculties to their limit.

No one, in recent times, at least, has stated this truth more clearly and more emphatically than that great Christian scientist, Père Teilhard de Chardin. I am not thinking so much of his *Phenomenon of Man* but of that other work of his, less well-known perhaps, but, in my opinion, much richer and profounder in content—*Le milieu divin*. The whole work is so filled and impregnated with the true spirit of the incarnation, that it is tempting to quote from it at great length. But we must content ourselves with two brief extracts:

> By virtue of the Creation and still more of the Incarnation, *nothing* here below is *profane* for those who know how to see. On the contrary, everything is sacred to the man who can distinguish that portion of chosen being which is subject to Christ's drawing power in the process of consummation. . . . What is sanctity in a creature if not to adhere to God with the maximum of his strength? And what does that maximum adherence to God mean if not the fulfilment—in the world organized around Christ—of the exact function, be it lowly or eminent, to which that creature is destined both by natural endowment and supernatural gift?

Again:

> Within the Church we observe all sorts of groups whose members are vowed to the perfect practice of this or that particular virtue. Why should there not be men vowed to the task of exemplifying by their lives the general sanctification of human endeavour?—Men whose common religious ideal would be to give a full and conscious explanation of the divine possibilities or demands which any worldly occupation implies—men, in a word, who would devote themselves, in the fields of thought, art, industry, commerce and politics, to carrying out in a sublime spirit these demands—the basic tasks which form the very skeleton of human society? Around us the "natural" progress which nourishes the sanctity of each new

age is all too often left to the children of this world, that is to say to agnostics and the irreligious. Unconsciously or involuntarily such men collaborate in the kingdom of God and in the fulfilment of the elect: their efforts, going beyond or correcting their incomplete or bad intentions, are gathered in by him whose energy "subjects all things to itself". But that is no more than a second best, a temporary phase in the organization of human activity. Right from the hands that knead the dough to those that consecrate it, the great and universal Host should be prepared and handled in a spirit of *adoration*.

That, surely, is sublimely said. What is there in such an ideal which should not attract rather than repel the genuine Humanist? For it means that man's special characteristics retain all their value and importance; but they acquire an added richness, a new dimension of value from their close association with the source and origin of all perfection and all power. In one sense, the teaching of Christianity leaves man exactly where the Humanist wants him to be—the master of his own fate, the controller of his own destiny; and yet, in another sense, it makes all the difference, because it means that man's achievement is not destined to perish with this world but has taken on a significance that carries it over into eternity. Which ideal really pays a greater compliment to man?

"But", the Humanist will doubtless retort, "there is really no evidence that what you are saying is *true,* even were I to grant you that it sounds all very well. Indeed," he might well go on to say, "your own position seems to rule out any possibility of your being able to defend or to justify your claims. If, as you say, it leaves man much where he was; if it means that the work of the scientist and the philosopher remains exactly as before; if the findings of the physicist and the chemist, the biologist and the psychologist provide the basic elements out of which man is to fashion his picture of the world, why should you introduce a factor which is, almost by your own definition, outside the range of these disciplines? I still fail to see where you get this idea of the supernatural from and what meaningful contribution it can possibly make to our understanding of reality since it manifestly falls outside what we normally mean by reality. Even were I to grant that, at the level of ordinary activity, there is no essential difference between my point of view and yours, why cannot you remain content with this picture, without introducing notions which, I must confess, seem to me nebulous and unsatisfactory from a purely rational point of view and, pragmatically tested, seem to add nothing at all, or nothing of any particular significance to man's understanding of himself and of his purpose in life?"

Perhaps we can start our discussion by looking at Sir Julian Huxley's term "god-hypothesis", to which reference has already been made. His use of the term implies that there is no sort of evidence by which this opinion can be tested. It remains a matter of opinion—an opinion which you cannot expect any scientific mind to accept. For the scientist can find acceptable only those truths which are capable of experimental verification. You see, when a scientist goes to work he usually starts from some hypothesis which helps him to control and direct his investigations. A hypothesis is, if you like, a sort of guess, but a guess which he subjects to various tests, by which he is able to justify it—or, it may be, sometimes to reject it. Take, for example, a simple illustration; the establishing of the boiling-point of water. Obviously, if you want to boil water, you must apply heat to it, as we all do when we put the kettle on. But the scientist discovers that water does not always boil at the same temperature. Roughly speaking water boils when it reaches a temperature of 212° Fahrenheit or 100° Centigrade, but this does not happen universally. Why is this so? Noticing that water boils at different temperatures according to the height above sea-level, some early investigator said, in effect: "My guess is that, as well as heat, atmospheric pressure has something to do with it." By a series of tests he is able to show that this is the case, and he is thus able to formulate more precisely the laws governing the boiling-point of water. When you show me what sort of experiments you have conducted to prove your god-hypothesis, I will begin to take it seriously.

Well now, let us look at this process a little more carefully. Obviously we accept the scientific procedure. But the question we want to ask is: how do you *explain* or prove what I may call your "hypothesis-hypothesis"? By which I mean this: if the only valid knowledge is derived from the testing of hypotheses (apart, of course, from direct observation) how do you arrive at this particular piece of knowledge? What hypothesis can you formulate, the testing of which can justify the whole scientific procedure you have just described? I can well imagine the scientist retorting, a little testily perhaps: "My dear chap, can't you see that the method justifies itself? Every time a hypothesis is tested and either established or rejected, the method itself acquires further convalidation. It is all, in the end, a matter of common-sense. That is obviously the way things are."

Of course it is. But equally obviously this argument shows that we do obtain knowledge by ways other than that of testing hypotheses. I think the simple-minded inquirer is justified in going on to ask: "When you say that that is the way things are, and that it is all a matter of common-sense, do you mean that that is the way things have always been? Or did that state of affairs come into existence with the emergence of the first human intelligence? I mean, did man invent this hypothesis-hypothesis or is it imposed on him by the way things are? Is it truer to say that the hypothesis-hypothesis is justified by the method or that it is the method which develops out of the way things are? Are you not, in fact, assuming something which is not patient of scientific proof, assuming the very basis of all scientific investigations? Are you not compelled by the facts to behave in this way, because no other way makes sense? I should, of course, entirely agree with you that it is all a matter of common-sense, but please don't expect me to be impressed by your pseudo-scientific talk about a 'god-hypothesis'. You maintain, justifiably, that science works because the scientist does his best to go along with the way things are, but this situation 'the way things are' is not itself capable of being itself made the subject matter of a hypothesis, otherwise you knock the whole bottom out of your own science, because you would never get started. So we believe that the existence of God is the ultimate ground for everything, including 'the way things are' not only in the world of scientific method, but also in the larger world of man's philosophical speculation, of his social relationships, his moral responsibilities, his aesthetic appreciation, and the like."

When the poet addresses God as "Ground of Being and granite of it", he is not indulging in a flight of fancy. He is making a statement about the way things are, in a sense much more fundamental than any scientific view of the world. Just as the scientist maintains that this scientific procedure is justified because it works, so we should claim that our belief in God is justified because it explains everything, including the rationality of the universe, which enables the scientist to achieve such remarkable results. The scientist's achievement is the outcome of his ability to find the answers to so many questions, raised by the human mind faced with the operations of this world. God, we should claim, is the Answer lying behind, implicit in, in a sense preceding the questions which the scientist asks. What this means is that, just as individual questions are asked by a human intelligence, so that without that intelligence no questions at all would get asked, so it seems necessary to postulate an order of intelligence, coming to consciousness *in us* by being *recognized,* but already self-conscious as all intelligence must be.

Doubtless the hard-bitten evolutionist would try to defend his position by asserting that mind did not exist until man existed, and that all that existed before man was mindless matter, chaotic and meaningless. At a given stage in the evolutionary process, to use Huxley's own language "Mind broke through"; but this, of course, is simply a misleading metaphor, begging the whole question. Things only break through—like chickens in an egg—when they are already there. How are we to conceive of the moment prior to this break-through? What precisely was on the way to breaking through? Presumably some sub-rational force existing, remember, in an irrational, meaningless world? Are we to think of pre-man as a kind of lunatic with lucid intervals, equivalently saying to himself: "Some of this makes sense, but some of it doesn't: but then I don't seem to make complete sense either. . . ." And, in any case, if the world before man was irrational, how can man, even when fully evolved, talk about it at all? Does he impose a pattern which was not there at all? Or does he discover a pattern which was there all the time, but was not recognized by any intelligence until man existed? Can you have a pattern at all, unless it is the outcome of some kind of system? Even the casual pattern made in the sand by the tide is only possible because of the nature of sand and the nature of water. If our knowledge of the structure of sand, of winds and waves and so on was sufficiently detailed, we should be able to forecast the patterns that would be produced in any given spot at any given moment. So we must not allow ourselves to be impressed by the famous, but fatuous, picture of the unintelligent ape sitting down at a typewriter and typing away through endless ages, with no conscious aim, but eventually producing the plays of Shakespeare. The fanatical evolutionist seems to suppose that so long as there is enough time, anything may happen. But we know very well that if we could investigate in its completeness the operation of the monkey's nervous and muscular system, we should be able to see how the result was produced—even if it was only one of the less inspired of Shakespeare's scenes—and we should be able to distinguish between that process and the process which produced the balcony scene in *Romeo and Juliet* or one of Hamlet's soliloquies.

What we are here concerned to do is not to score debating points against the evolutionist but to bring out the important truth that the position of the theist is far more *rational,* far more *intelligent* than is that of the evolutionary Humanist. We do not deny that there are immense and mysterious problems to be faced in the idea of God. But at least we do not end up in irrationality, in a denial of the very foundations of our faith, which is what the evolutionist surely does. Moreover, even accepting, for the purpose of argument, the scientist's demand that we should regard the existence of God as a hypothesis requiring justification by empirical observation, the following facts seem to be highly relevant.

If God does not exist, how are we to explain the certain truth that the vast majority of mankind has from the beginning assumed that he does? Not alone the mystics and the metaphysicians, but average men and women have held that there is some reality beyond this present world, however little they may have allowed this idea to influence their day-to-day behaviour. How much of man's time and energy have been devoted to religious worship, to the building of temples and churches and other places consecrated to some religious belief or other, to the portrayal in painting and sculpture and letters of some religious ideal. These are empirical facts, inexplicable on the view that mankind has to this extent been utterly misled.

The die-hard sceptic will, of course, try to refute this argument by pointing to the generations of men who have believed that the earth stood still and that the sun went round it, that the earth was flat and not spherical, and so on. But there is no substance in this argument either, once you really examine it. For, of course, the views of the flat-earthers and of the fixed-earthers do serve to explain the facts up to an important point. When you open your *Times* it tells you what time the sun rises and sets, without any footnote saying that, of course, it doesn't really rise and set, since it is truer to say that the earth sets and rises with reference to the sun. If you ask a motoring organization for a route, they will tell you that certain stretches of the road are level. They don't qualify this by saying that, of course, there is a slight but undetectable curve on even the most level surface.

So, up to an important point, the scientist explains the facts. But we must not allow him to get away with the suggestion that we believers are no better than flat-earthers, believing in a system which has been refuted by subsequent discoveries. It is the sceptic who is the flat-earther, refusing to accept anything that cannot be verified by his own experience. Just as the Copernican astronomer has enlarged our appreciation of what the solar system as a whole, and therefore this planet, is really like, without discrediting the findings of the ordinary man's experience so, we should maintain, belief in God does not do away with anything that science may have established but sees it simply as an incomplete and inadequate statement of what reality as a whole is like.

There is still validity in the argument of Socrates in the *Phaedo,* rejecting the "scientific behaviourism" of Anaxagoras:

> He seemed to me to have fallen exactly into the predicament of a man who, maintaining generally that Mind is the cause of the actions of Socrates, should then, when he undertook to explain my conduct in detail, go on to show that I sit here because my body is made up of bones and muscles; and the bones, as he would say, are hard and have joints which divide them, and the muscles are elastic and so on. . . . He would have a similar explanation of my talking to you, which he would attribute to sound and air, and hearing; and he would assign a thousand other causes of the same sort, neglecting to mention the true cause, which is that the Athenians have thought fit to condemn me, and accordingly I have thought it better and more right to remain here and undergo my sentence: for if it were just a question of my bones and muscles, they would have looked after themselves and betaken themselves long ago to Megara or Boeotia, if I had not thought it better and nobler not to play truant and run away, but rather to remain here and undergo any punishment the state may inflict. . . . If anyone wants to say that unless I had bones and muscles and the rest of my body, I could not perform what I want to do, that is reasonable enough; but to say that I act as I do because of them, and that this is the way my mind acts, and not from choice of the best, why, that is a very careless and futile way of speaking.

How can any evolutionary theory explain or justify the behaviour of a Socrates? It has to be an extremely modified form of natural selection which would make it feasible to argue that, by dying, Socrates helped to produce a higher type of man than had previously existed. For on any empirical view of human history what happened was that Socrates was put to death because certain inferior individuals, who happened to have the power, got their way. The Athenian empire came to an end, the civilization, of which Socrates was such a bright ornament, withered, and his example was preserved, not by any immediate response on the part of individuals who began to lead a better life, but because his story was preserved for posterity in manuscript form, to help man to keep alive certain ideals which he somehow appreciates, but which are not kept in being by any recognizable or continuous chain, composed of links in an ascending order of value. While it is, alas, regrettably true that men have often failed to live up to their highest ideals, this is at least intelligible and explicable in terms of human experience. What is not explicable on any theory of natural selection which can be described as scientific (in the narrow sense of the word) is *how* these ideals are preserved and improved on.

Once again, as in the case of man's intellectual development, so in the case of his moral experience, the Christian view of things seems to be more sensible, less self-contradictory than the baffling and literally incredible explanations attempted by the Humanist. For, while the latter seems prepared to concede to human beings a capacity for creation out of nothing which he denies to any other being, creating mind out of matter, creating truth out of nonsense, creating morality out of its complete absence, the Christian argues that the very terms true and false, good and bad and so on are intelligible and meaningful only with reference to some absolute standard whose existence, by his own logic, the Humanist is compelled to deny.

Mysterious as are the processes of human thought, subtle and difficult of analysis as is man's moral awareness and aesthetic appreciation, it is not just reason and logic, it is the very process of human history and the facts of man's experience which seem to be much more on the side of the Christian interpretation than on the Humanist's dogmatic denial of its validity. It is only in terms of Christian truth that the noblest ideals of Humanism find their justification.

There is a passage in Tolstoy's *War and Peace* which is appropriate here.

> You say you cannot see the kingdom of goodness and truth on earth. Neither have I seen it: nor is it possible for any one to see it who looks upon this life as the sum and end of all. . . . Do not I feel that in this countless company of beings, wherein the Divinity is manifested, I make one link, one step between the lower being and the higher? If I see, and clearly see, the ladder leading from plant to man, then why must I suppose that it breaks off at me, and does not lead on further and beyond? . . . If God and the future life exist, then truth and virtue exist; and man's highest happiness consists in striving for their attainment. . . .

If, then, we Christians hold that in Christianity alone is to be found the justification for the Humanist's idealism, it is not that we reject that idealism as false; it is that we refuse to believe that it is an adequate version of the truth. For man's own sake, we plead for a recognition of the fuller truth and fuller nobility of our version of man's destiny. There may well be a sense in which the evolution doctrine is a kind of mirror-image, a two-dimensional representation of a reality that is three-dimensional. Or, to vary the picture, the Humanist sees the world-process like the development of the heliotrope, striving towards a sun which is not there. The Christian explains the process in terms of a two-way traffic, the sun giving life and warmth to enable the heliotrope to return to its source and origin, in a striving which is not doomed to eternal frustration—as the Humanist would hold—but the success of which is assured, if only man will play his part. If such a view does not set a higher worth on all human striving, then I would gladly renounce Christianity and throw in my lot with the Humanists. But I know that the Christian teaching about man must be the richest and truest possible. For it states that man is the object of the Infinite Love of Uncreated Beauty. What a shoddy thing by comparison is the Humanist creed which would regard man as the object of the self-love of essential imperfection.

As Socrates said long ago, in *The Laws:* "Neither you nor your friends are the first to hold atheistical opinions; there have always been plenty of people suffering from this disease. . . ." So we should like to say to the Humanist: "You are not the first to hold that, because man is the noblest creature that falls within our purview, there cannot be any thing nobler." Yet, surely, the very nobility of his greatest achievements is enhanced by the recognition that there is that which is Nobility itself. Listen, then, we should like to ask them, to the noble testimony of Augustine, who came at last to see that the Humanist ideal was not enough:

Not with doubting but with conscious certainty do I love thee, O Lord. The heavens, too, and the earth and everything it contains, all about me on every side clearly bids me love thee. . . . But what do I love, when I love thee? Not bodily grace nor the changing beauty of the seasons nor the brightness of light that so delights the eye: not the undying melody of pleasing song, nor the sweet fragrance of flowers, of unguents and spices, not manna and honey, nor limbs that give delight in the body's embracing. None of these do I love in loving my God. And yet, it is a kind of light that I love, a kind of melody, a kind of fragrance; in a way it is food, as it is the rapture of embracing that I enjoy in enjoying my God; the embracing, the food, the fragrance, melody and light known to my inmost self, in which there shines upon my soul a light which space cannot contain, where there is a melody that time cannot snatch away, a fragrance which the wind's breath does not disperse, a taste that does not cloy the palate, a close embrace that does not know satiety and separation. This is it which I love when I love my God.

What then is it? I asked the earth, which said: I am not he; and all that is on earth made the same confession. I asked the sea and the deeps and all that swims or moves in that habitation: and they answered: We are not thy God, seek above us. I asked the wandering winds, and the whole air with all its inhabitants who replied: Anaximenes was deceived, I am not thy God. I asked the heavens, the sun and moon and stars and I received back the reply: We are not the God of your search. And I made answer unto all these things which encompass the portals of my flesh: Ye have told me of my God that ye are not he: tell me something about him. And they cried out, all with a great voice: He made us. My questioning them was my mind's desire, and their answer was their beauty.

He will, I fear, not thank us for saying so; but this is really what the Humanist is after all the time. The sad thing is that he has been a better guide to us than we have always been to him.

PART II

THE CHRISTIAN AS PHILOSOPHER

CHAPTER V

REASON AND FAITH

It is, presumably, an indication of the limited nature of human intelligence that men of integrity, insight and genuine intellectual ability are yet so often found in mutual disagreement. Men who have a great desire to arrive at truth, who go to immense pains to study what they can discover of the relevant evidence can nevertheless come to widely diverging conclusions about the same subject matter. This sad reflection is prompted by the perennial conflict between believer and non-believer, between, say, Christian and Humanist. There can be no doubt at all of the Humanist's desire to establish the truth; there can be no sort of doubt that he is a staunch and valuable warrior in the unceasing battle for truth; all who cherish human reason will welcome him as an ally. And yet the sad fact remains that, in this matter of the relationship between reason and faith, he has so regrettably failed.

Not that there are not many explanations of and reasons for that failure: not that many Catholics have not given utterance to ideas which justify much of his condemnation. But when I reflect on the great role which the Catholic Church has played in the defence of that reason which the Humanist so rightly seeks to uphold, when I think of the countless man-years which Catholic scholars have devoted to rational pursuits of one sort or another I cannot but feel sorry that it should be necessary once again to labour points which are, to thinking Catholics, so banal as to be boring, so primitive as to be platitudinous.

St Peter, in his first Epistle, told the faithful: ". . . be ready always to give an answer to any man that asketh you

a reason of the hope that is in you . . ." and this insistence
on the reasonableness of belief, echoed elsewhere in the New
Testament, has always been a feature of Christian and Catholic theological and philosophical speculation. It is a common-
place of Catholic teaching that philosophy, the rational investigation of human experience, is the handmaid of theology.
Reason and faith together produce a being who tries to live
a full life, and is helped to live that full life because he believes that he is given an insight into a truth that is beyond
the reach of unaided reason and yet is wholly consonant with
and indeed integrated into truth rationally apprehended. It
is as though, by reason, he could only know truth in a two-
dimensional way, while faith introduces him to a three-
dimensional world; but this three-dimensional world is built
upon, is in a real sense a continuation and development of,
the two-dimensional. The cube does not exist apart from its
plane sides; faith does not exist apart from reason. Nor can
faith dispense with reason, act as a substitute for it; still less
is there any conflict between the findings of the two.

Indeed, it is a fact, not sufficiently appreciated by many,
even among those belonging to the Church itself, that the
very meaning and content of the faith is to a very large extent
controlled and even developed by rational methods. This
historical process by which the great dogmas of the faith
were elaborated is surely a magnificent tribute to the work of
patient reasoned investigation, demanding a great equipment
of scholarship. Let me refer, by way of illustration, to the
masterly work of a French Jesuit, Père Lebreton, which bears
the title *Les Origines du dogme de la Trinité*. Even a cursory
study of this volume ought to dispose of the notion that
Catholics imagine that revelation is something that just happens, like a thunderbolt out of a clear sky, with no previous
preparation and no relation to normal human thought-
processes. Lebreton shows how, into a ferment of hellenistic
philosophical and religious ideas, already mingling in Philo
with a current of thought deriving from the great teachers
of Judaism, the teaching of the New Testament was injected,

to produce over a period of centuries the precise formularies
of the Creed. Yet, while the process is a genuinely historical
affair, patient of historical and philosophical investigation, it
differs from the process by which, for example, the principles
of Communism were crystallized by Marx, Lenin and Stalin.
They, while they influence the course of history, are yet
themselves entirely within it. Jesus Christ, God and man, is
at once part of, yet, just as truly, standing over and above the
stream of temporal happenings.

It may help to elucidate our problem if we investigate the
way in which the Catholic looks at this central truth and
mystery of his faith—the doctrine of the incarnation. It will
make for greater clarity if we investigate the matter in two
ways. We shall think, first, of the way in which that truth is
held by someone who has been brought up in the faith from
childhood. We shall then look at the case of the unbeliever
who comes to accept it. The average Catholic child is
"taught" to believe in the incarnation as he is taught the facts
of history, geography and mathematics. Somebody called
William, Duke of Normandy, invaded England in the year
1066, defeated Harold at the Battle of Hastings and became
King of England: Everest is the highest mountain in the
world: a number, the sum of whose digits is divisible by 3
is itself divisible by 3: Jesus Christ is God and man. All
these statements are accepted as true, not because there is
any obvious intrinsic reason why they should be, but because
people who are apparently trustworthy say they are true.
For some years that is the way in which further truths are
acquired.

Then comes the stage at which it is possible for the child to
investigate these matters for himself. In the case of William
the Conqueror, the student is given some idea of historical
method, though it probably remains true to say that he con-
tinues to accept the statement because it fits into a general
pattern which is the background of his thought. Everybody
who writes about English history accepts the story of 1066
at its face value. The motives impelling the different actors

in the story to behave as they did become matter for dispute; the basic fact is unchallenged. The student begins to see that history is pieced together from fragmentary bits of evidence, the very shifts in emphasis and interpretation serving somehow to strengthen his conviction of the general truth of the story as a whole. He may have the good fortune to come across a book like Miss Josephine Tey's brilliant discussion of the story of the murder of the Princes in the Tower. He will see that historians may have been a little too credulous about the villainy of Richard III. He will not, if he is wise, conclude that history is bunk; he will not begin to wonder whether perhaps there never were any Princes to be murdered, whether perhaps it is unsafe to trust historians at all. The very process of historical criticism is enough to guarantee the essential soundness of historical opinions. A bit of the mosaic has been corrected; the mosaic as a whole remains.

Let us turn now to the doctrine of the incarnation. By this time our student has begun to think for himself about the truths of his faith as well. He *may,* of course, meet with a stupid or timid teacher who says: "Truths of faith are different from other truths; you must not examine *them;* you must just accept them." If that happens, then the chances are that his faith will be disturbed, because he has reached the age at which it is natural and right that he should ask questions. If he is more fortunate, he will be shown the reasons why we do believe in the incarnation. He will be given some idea of the historical evidence for the existence of Jesus Christ; he will be shown how the details of the New Testament record fit into the pattern derived from other sources, how Tacitus quite unexpectedly underwrites an odd detail or two of the Gospel story, how the findings of archeology corroborate the story of the Acts, how, in a word, the story of Jesus Christ is rooted in history. Where the New Testament writings can be submitted to the ordinary process of historical investigation they come out well enough to justify him in believing in their authenticity.

The argument then shifts to a consideration of the character of this man. The impression he made on his contemporaries, to judge by what we know of early Christian history, was at least as remarkable as was that made by Socrates, say, on his friends and disciples. Now very few people who are at all interested in the matter will refuse to credit Socrates with a character of great integrity and moral worth, partly on the quality of his teaching, partly on the estimate of his friends. Not less, surely, is to be attributed to Christ on the strength of similar evidence. But the argument now moves to a higher level. For there is about *this* man a curiously novel and somewhat disturbing feature. He is either inferior to his fellowmen or he is in some mysterious way immensely superior. He makes claims which, if they are not valid, suggest that he is a megalomaniac or a charlatan: but if they are valid then he is a being unique in human history. For he claims an equality with the divine Father who sent him.

Is the claim valid? And here, perhaps, we may turn to our other investigator—the man who has not been brought up to accept the doctrine of the incarnation on authority at first, afterwards submitting the doctrine to rational test. We shall think of the not infrequent case of the man brought up in paganism or unbelief, who in later life encounters Christianity and examines its credentials. He is not asked to begin by accepting the doctrine on faith, by making a submission to authority. He is expected, indeed required, to look at the evidence as unemotionally and rationally as possible, to see the figure of Christ against its historical background, to read the story of his life, death and resurrection. This is the crux of the matter. If the resurrection happened, then the matter is beyond argument. The rest follows. But how can we know that the resurrection happened? Some of the line of argument we have already developed is relevant here—the support which the New Testament record receives from contemporary historians and from archaeological evidence, the sublimity of Christ's teaching, the witness of his friends and followers. It will be necessary, of course, to investigate the authenticity of the existing records, to show by the ordinary use of evidence,

internal and external, that a *prima facie* case can be made
out in support of the view that the Gospels were written in
the half-century following the events they purport to describe,
that the Epistles of St Paul are, in part at least, still earlier
than the Gospels, that these writers were men who at least
believed what they narrated. The written evidence for the
resurrection will be scrutinized with particular care, and the
events of the first decades of Christian history studied in
relation to all the evidence available from non-Christian
historians.

At this stage, it may be useful to propound alternative
hypotheses—the hypothesis that the Christian writers were
misguided or were deliberately lying and the hypothesis that
these accounts are true. Which hypothesis squares better with
the evidence we possess? If the latter hypothesis is shown to
be more probable and no better hypothesis can be formed,
it will be necessary for the honest inquirer to accept it and to
act on it. This means that, since the hypothesis now becomes
a working hypothesis it must be applied to certain test situations. It will appear, for example, that the history of Europe
at certain specific moments has been profoundly modified
by the actions of men who believed in the "hypothesis".
It will be seen that the lives of countless individuals have
been enormously affected in the same way. The hypothesis
is ceasing to be a hypothesis, a theory: it is becoming a matter
of urgent personal concern. At this stage the inquirer is
called upon to make a decision. Does he or does he not accept
the Christian story as true? If he does, then, for him, the
whole pattern of his life and the whole significance of human
history is changed. He has committed himself to the acceptance of far more than a set of propositions to be proved
or disproved by scientific investigation or logical analysis.
He has accepted, for perfectly valid logical reasons, a whole
picture of history and a philosophy of life, which takes him
straightway beyond the realms of physics and biology, of
psychology and logic, into a world of ideas which clearly

stem from and support his normal ideas, yet are not deduced from normal experience as his normal ideas are. His natural self and his naturally-derived notions are not suppressed or rendered less significant. Only a whole new dimension has been added to life. These higher truths which he has come to accept are not discontinuous or at variance with his purely rational convictions. On the contrary his everyday ideas seem to have become themselves invested with a profounder meaning. It is as though he had been groping about in a dark room, painfully and slowly accumulating information about its contents by the feel of them. Now a light has been switched on, revealing new objects and illuminating the old. Nothing has been lost; an immense amount has been gained. Revelation has come in to complete the picture elaborated by reason.

It is unnecessary to pursue the line of argument further. Let us rather break off and see how it applies to the general theme of this chapter. I have been arguing for the view that to have faith in Catholic truth is not only not incompatible with reason; it *demands* reason. But equally it implies that reason is not enough. Reason is not enough because reason is not enough for life at the ordinary level. The man who tries to reduce truth to a series of propositions is in danger of turning life into a "ghostly ballet of bloodless categories". It is enough for me to have had a certain measure of experience of another person's way of behaving to be able to form an opinion of that person's character which will be beyond the reach of hostile criticism. If I have known a friend long enough then, no matter how many the accusations levelled against him, how black the evidence may seem to be, if it is incompatible with the opinion I have come to form from adequate experience, it is not irrational of me to say: "I believe in him, in spite of this or that bit of evidence." It is not irrational of me to say: "I cannot understand how to reconcile this evidence with his innocence; but I am certain that there *is* an explanation." Here some factor has come into play which, while not contradicting reason, while indeed based on rational estimates, yet goes beyond what mere reason can avail.

Now when we turn back to the Catholic notion of faith, this extra "factor" is what we call the super-natural. What that term means will take some little time to elucidate, would indeed require a whole chapter for adequate treatment. For our purposes, it may suffice to point out that a reasonable attitude to all the evidence available suggests that there is an order of reality higher than that of which we have direct experience in sense-awareness, higher even than that activity of the human reason which we call thought. Let me put it this way. My pet dog presumably lives a life of successive awareness of things about him that feel what we call wet or hard, taste bitter or sweet, smell attractively or not, and so on. That group of things includes *me*—a caressing hand, a pair of boots with an individual smell, a unique shape. . . . From my point of view, these aspects of me are far from important. I treasure much more my ability to read, to discuss literature with my friends, to listen to music, to think, to do a whole lot of things which I not merely cannot communicate to my dog, but which are beyond the range of his experience. They are completely above what his nature is made for, is capable of. He is aware of me, because I can produce sensations in him. But what makes me most truly myself remains inscrutable for him.

Now Catholics believe that, in an analogous way, there is is a whole realm of activity beyond the scope of human nature as such. They believe in God, and in a God who can and does act upon their consciousness in various ways— specifically, for our present purpose, by revelation. It seems to us not unreasonable to think that, just as poets and artists are stirred and moved by impulses which do not seem to be of their deliberate choosing, so prophets and teachers may be used by God as instruments to enlighten men's minds in special directions and for special purposes. This is no place to enter into the mechanics of the business. Only, we think, granted God, the rest seems to follow. We hold, too, that, under a special guiding care, the sacred books of the Jews were preparing mankind, in a representative section, for further and fuller revelations. These were finally made by a human being, called Jesus Christ, in a life of remarkable integrity, sublime ethical teaching and unusual powers over nature. It is not impossible to bring arguments against this or that feature of the story of Christ's life. But there can be little doubt now, after the fierce scrutiny of the past century, that it is far more reasonable to accept the substantial truth of the story as a whole and of its particular details, than to reject it outright. But, unless you reject it outright, you seem to be committed to accept what Christ taught, simply because he, a man of obvious integrity and intelligence, did teach it. You are, surely, committed to accept his teaching on his authority. The alternative is to prefer your own judgement about ultimate truth to his.

In his valuable work, *The Nature of Thought,* Professor Blanshard has tried to show that authority is valueless as a source of truth. He poses a dilemma: a man who accepts pronouncements as authoritative may give reasons for his acceptance or he may not. If he gives reasons then he is, equivalently, re-introducing reason as the ultimate ground and rejecting authority. If he does not give reasons, certain intolerable consequences follow. But surely there is a certain confusion in the former member of this dilemma. The fact that I can adduce reasons for accepting a certain authority does not mean that those reasons are the ground of my believing whatever that authority says. I could, I suppose, draw up a list of the reasons why I accept the authority of a railroad time-table. They would include my own personal experience of its reliability, the fact that it is commonly accepted by others, the obvious truth that it would not pay the publishers to bring out a misleading time-table. But when I consult it my *sole* reason for believing that a certain train is due to leave at a certain time is my belief in the time-table's reliability.

Belief in a person's reliability is, of course, a much more complex and subtle affair. The whole process by which I come to *know* another person at all intimately involves immensely varied and intricately interconnected factors, in which reason plays an important but by no means exclusive part. It requires, for example, the whole business of emotional response to another's friendliness, the whole sense of kinship between human personalities, the need we all have of communion with another. I do not apply rational tests to my responses. I may, indeed, say: this is a foolish, or a dangerous, or a healthy, or an inspiring affection. I may succeed, at times, in "controlling" my impulses by "reason". But, on the whole, on a basis of reason, I allow my impulses to lead to a deepening of a relationship which would be but a poor shadow of a thing if it were a merely rational and carefully thought-out affair. Love is just not that sort of experience. And, where reason is not ruled out, where, on the contrary, love comes in to reinforce and enrich the findings of reason, we have a love which is not blind but clear-sighted, which really gives us more information about another person's character and personality than any merely scientific investigation could. Are we then to say that such a love is irrational because it cannot be dissected or analysed by the logician or described in neat formularies or made the subject of a philosophical lecture? Is poetry irrational? Or, if it is, does that condemn poetry, or reason? There is an art of friendship, a poetry of love which not all the syllogisms of all the philosophers will destroy. And if I seek to explain or to justify to another my love of a friend, if my explanation is intelligible or my justification convincing, the chances are that I shall myself find them unsatisfactory and displeasing.

If this is the truth (or something like it) about human love, how immensely, indeed immeasurably truer must it be of religious faith. For here we have personal communion at its highest and purest, mediated of course by material factors, coloured and warmed by art and emotion, supported and directed by reason, yet reaching heights and depths beyond the reach of either emotion or reason. "Who can speak of eternity without a solecism or think thereof without an ecstasy?" It follows, then, that any attempt to defend it, since such defence must be couched in the language of argument, must prove inadequate. Yet the attempt must be made. What then are we to say of the Catholic's attitude to his faith? In the first place, he understands that it is not primarily a matter of intellectual appreciation. Faith is a decision of the will, based on an intellectual process, but going far beyond what the intellect can understand. He sees enough to satisfy him that, in making the surrender of his will, he is not stultifying himself. That he should believe seems to him entirely reasonable, even though what he is called upon to believe is far beyond the reach of reasoned argument. In fact it seems to him entirely reasonable that there should exist truths beyond the scope of his mind. For what he believes is nothing less than the truth about God, about creation, about himself. A decent modesty might prompt him to reflect that he hardly could hope to understand all that. He finds himself baffled in his attempt to understand the everyday world about him; it seems to him therefore most probable that, when he comes to reflect on the world beyond this, he should encounter mystery.

Using his reason as far as it will go, studying such evidence as is available to him, he comes to what is for him the inevitable conclusion—that religion has to be taken seriously. God exists. That fact alone matters. Or if other facts matter, they matter only relatively to it. Convinced that God exists and that his own existence is secondary to and dependent upon God, he has no difficulty in supposing that the truth about himself, about life, about the world, is to be sought somehow from God. He finds himself normally living in a group or a family which accepts, as from God, a whole range of statements which form a satisfying and coherent system. It is just not true, as has been alleged, that he finds himself committed to holding truths which are mutually inconsistent and contradictory. There may be many occasions on which he comes up against statements which seem, at first sight, difficult to reconcile one with the other. When that happens, he goes to work patiently, rationally, to find out more fully what they mean. For he knows that truth is one and indivisible. He calls to his aid the findings of science and history, of psychology and literary criticism to resolve the problem. His faith tells him that there is a solution. It is by use of his reason that he hopes to find it.

Take, for example, the much-canvassed question of biblical inerrancy. The Catholic does indeed hold that the words of scripture, being divinely inspired, cannot be misleading. Does that mean, therefore, that he takes apparent contradictions at their face value and seeks refuge in blind faith? Where some passage in the Bible is apparently at variance with scientifically established fact, does he say: so much the worse for science? Not at all. When, for example, Joshua prays for the sun to stand still, implicitly denying, it would seem, the Copernican system, the Catholic remembers that we all equally implicitly deny the Copernican system when we talk about the rising or the setting of the sun. The Bible is talking that sort of language. It is not addressing a meeting of the Royal Astronomical Society. It is, of course, an undeniable fact that some of Europe's most distinguished astronomers have been devout and convinced Catholics. Copernicus was a Catholic priest; and even Galileo was a convinced, if not necessarily a devout, Catholic. Had he shown a little more tact, he would have had less trouble with the authorities. If they had shown a little more wisdom and a little more humility, they would have done the Church a much greater service. In the end, the problem of Galileo is a psychological and historical one rather than a profoundly important theological one. There is no denying and no need to deny that the Church authorities lost their heads a bit about Galileo. But only those who have not bothered to read up the evidence can make out much of a case against the Church's fundamental sympathy with the scientific mentality. The average Catholic knows perfectly well that the list of Catholic scientists is long enough to make nonsense of any such accusation. He knows perfectly well, too, that if he rejects the Church's authority he is not likely to find any better guide through the perplexities of human existence. There are details in the system which puzzle him; there are demands made upon him which he does not always entirely relish. There will be times when he wishes desperately that the whole thing were not true. He has to confess, a little wryly, that when he is accused, as he is accused, of wishful thinking in thus accepting God and the Church, he cannot help feeling that wishful thinking would have produced a less exacting form of discipline.

For, of course, faith does make demands. Wholeheartedly accepted and seriously lived, it requires constant vigilance and a constant effort at growth. It is simply untrue that the Catholic faith is a series of antiquated, rigid and rather meaningless propositions, to be accepted in a spirit of blind and uncritical acquiescence. So alive and actual is it, that only by a corresponding vital effort can the Catholic hope to live up to it. Hence it is possible for him to fail to increase in stature in accordance with its requirements, to grow away from instead of into the faith, to lose touch with it to such an extent that it does become a burden rather than an inspiration. Properly accepted it is a skeleton which gives shape and strength to his life: but not a skeleton in a cupboard. If at times the Catholic is made to feel a little out of date because he has not read the latest book on biblical criticism, preferring, it may be, to read the Bible itself, he will not worry about that unless he is an intellectual snob. He rests in the secure belief that no sort of truth can conflict with the word of Truth itself, which is the content of his faith.

For the Catholic believes what he believes not just because he is told to believe by the Church authorities, any more than the good citizen keeps the law just because there is a policeman at hand to enforce its observance. Behind the policeman is the authority of the state, acting for the common good; behind the Church authorities is God. One common misrepre-

sentation of the Catholic position is the statement that
Catholics are not encouraged or even allowed to read the
Bible. This certainly is untrue. Not only is a Catholic encouraged and expected to study and read the Bible privately,
but extracts from it form considerable parts of the liturgy at
which he assists. What is true is that the Church values the
Bible so highly that she will not allow irresponsible criticism
and interpretation of its contents. Just as the law and constitution of the civil state is safeguarded by the work of experts upon it, and nothing but confusion and anarchy could
result if "private judgement" were given its head in that
sphere, so does the Church hold that the immensely subtle
points of doctrine contained or implied in the Bible literature
need to be studied and interpreted by those who are most
competent in the matter. There is sound Catholic sense in
the remark of Oliver Goldsmith: "As I take my shoes from
the shoemaker and my coat from the tailor, so I take my
religion from the priest." The Catholic knows that, where
points of faith are concerned, no man is adequately equipped
to pronounce a verdict, and he is content to allow the patient
work of the scholar, controlled and directed by the wisdom
and experience of the age-old Church, to elucidate for him
the sense of the words of Moses and the prophets, of Christ
and his apostles.

In virtue of his faith, then, the Catholic moves about in
worlds not realized, and for that reason may at times seem
to be out of touch with what is called reality. It must be so,
when human beings attempt to relate the temporal to the
eternal, the visible to the invisible, the natural to the supernatural. The Catholic is convinced that the natural can be
the vehicle for the supernatural. That fact alone should
deepen his reverence for it. Thus natural reason is the vehicle
for supernatural revelation. Therefore, in the great task of
defending human reason against every sort of assault upon it,
the contribution of the Catholic Church has been formidable.
Intellectum valde ama, "Have a great love for the human
intellect", has ever been her bidding. For she knows that

a man will come to faith in God only by using such wits as God has given to him, although she knows too that you cannot go all the way simply by reason.

I remember with much joy an amusing fourth leader which appeared in *The Times* some years ago, based on the discovery by an electricity-meter reader that some good soul had consumed during the quarter an infinitesimally small amount of current. Investigation followed; when questioned, the lady admitted that she used electricity only to enable her to see to fill her old-fashioned oil-lamp, which was her normal means of illumination. Not for her these new-fangled ways, though to be sure they had their uses. Now I venture to suggest that those who look askance at revelation and think that, somehow, it is inferior to reason are behaving rather like that old lady. Oil-lamps are all very well; but they have a limited effectiveness. Failing electricity, they will serve. But it is curiously reactionary to believe that, as sources of illumination, they are somehow better than electric lights. Similarly, reason is an admirable power, to be used to the full. But revelation gives an immense depth and fullness and richness to our outlook, far and away beyond the capacity of unaided reason.

May I, at this stage, quote some words from Newman—no one has written more profoundly or more tellingly on this subject: "Revealed Religion begins," he says

> where Natural Religion fails. The religion of Nature is a mere inchoation, and needs a complement—it can have but one complement, and that very complement is Christianity. . . . Thus it is that Christianity is the fulfilment of the promise made to Abraham and of the Mosaic revelations; this is how it has been able from the first to occupy the world and gain a hold on every class of human society to which its preachers reached; this is why the Roman power and the multitudes of religions which it embraced could not stand against it; this is the secret of its sustained energy and its never-flagging martyrdoms; this is how at present it is so mysteriously potent, in spite of the new and fearful adversaries which beset its path. It has with it that gift of staunching and healing the one deep wound of human nature, which avails more and more for

its success than a full encyclopedia of scientific knowledge and a whole library of controversy, and therefore, it must last while human nature lasts. It is a living truth which never can grow old.

I am aware how much criticism in detail can be brought against this or that aspect of Catholic life. I am aware how often timidity and lack of faith have beset those who should have gone forward in confident pursuit of fuller knowledge. No Catholic who reads history with attention and impartiality can fail to be astonished at the prejudice and ignorance, the short-sightedness and intellectual dishonesty displayed by far too many of his fellow-Catholics, or to contrast with these the singlemindedness and integrity which non-Catholic scholars have so often and so conspicuously manifested. But when the worst has been said, when the cess-pools have been plumbed and the whited sepulchres opened, it remains incontestably true that the roll of Catholic thinkers and scholars, scientists and historians is impressive and convincing. If the Catholic Church were the compound of charlatanry and chicanery, obscurantism and oppression, ignorance and intolerance which she is sometimes made out to be, could she have survived the onslaught of the centuries? Let us remember that it was she who tamed the Frank and civilized the Vandal, who preserved for posterity the legacies of Greece and Rome, who gave to Europe its universities and filled them with her teachers. My own university chose for its motto: *Dominus illuminatio mea*. What arrogance there would be in the words, did they not imply the humble recognition that, when human reason has reached its limit, the final radiance comes, not from the fitful lamps of man's fashioning but from the unfailing light of the eternal, in whose light we shall, at length, see light.

CHAPTER VI

THE PHENOMENON OF TEILHARD DE CHARDIN

The reception accorded to the published works of Teilhard de Chardin has been almost bewildering in its diversity. The professional philosophers have been most forthright, not to say vitriolic, in condemnation; the theologians have been chilly, suspicious or at best hesitant; scientists have been generally sympathetic, with Sir Julian Huxley's Introduction to the English edition of *The Phenomenon of Man* leading the chorus of praise. But it is, above all, the educated layman who has found in these writings inspiration and hope. Perhaps the time has come to try to form some estimate of the significance of the work of such a controversial figure.

In the first place, we easily recognize why the contemporary philosopher shows himself so hostile to the thought of such a writer. His language is at the opposite pole to that of the rigid clinical surgeon of linguistic analysis, whose ambition seems to be to reduce the processes of human thinking to something approximating to those of a mechanical brain. But this is not the way in which, as a rule, the greatest thinkers have operated, and it seems right to argue that the contribution of modern philosophers to the store of human achievement has not been conspicuously progressive. They may have provided a brake on exuberance, but it seems unlikely that the last half-century will be thought of as one of the most prosperous periods in the long history of philosophical speculation. We need not, then, regard the strictures of the philosophers as necessarily damaging to the reputation of Teilhard.

It is more important to look at the reaction of the theologians. After all, Teilhard was a priest, with a professional responsibility for the Church's dogmatic teaching and if it could be shown that his ideas were at variance with that teaching, this would indeed be much more damaging. The chief reason why his writings were originally denied publication and why, after publication, they were considered unsuitable for general dissemination, is presumably owing to a failure to appreciate his purpose in writing the work on which he has tended to be judged—*The Phenomenon of Man*. As the very title implies, he is looking at man phenomenologically, as a feature, if indeed the most important feature, of the world of our ordinary perceptions. He is trying to explain man and man's development in terms of his natural environment, knowing all the time that the whole explanation is not to be found there.

But it is unfair to treat *The Phenomenon* as if it were a theological study. It is a study addressed to the man of science—whether the professional scientist or the typical product of a scientific age. Of course, as he himself made clear in the occasional footnotes to *The Phenomenon*— footnotes which have not received the attention they merit— he knew that the whole story could not be told in purely scientific, this-world terms. But how is one to appeal to men whose whole cast of thought, language and imagery are limited to the phenomenological order? The great teachers of truth, beginning with Christ himself, have always tried to adapt themselves to the limitations of their hearers, and if, inevitably, this has led to some economy of the truth, this must not be ascribed to dishonesty or ignorance.

Certainly, the success of his appeal to men who think almost instinctively in evolutionary terms can hardly be overestimated. If today the scientific humanist is prepared to listen with anything approaching tolerance to the utterance of Christian thinkers, this fact must be ascribed in no small measure to the pioneer work of one who never concealed his deepest beliefs yet could command respect as a scientist in his own right.

Professor de Terra has this to say:

> I am aware that Teilhard's visionary and religious strength puts him in a special position. That is to say, the humanism engendered by science need not necessarily derive from the specific blend of religious and scientific experience which was characteristic of Teilhard. Even though he considered this desirable, his works do not convey a note of flat insistence. The very fact that he looked upon the science of man as a prime means of understanding evolution indicates that he aimed at a *universal* acceptance of his ideas. He was thinking of a "human front", a mobilization of individually-based knowledge of the origin and destiny of man. His theories were meant to be accessible not only to members of his own or other denominations, but to all. . . . Teilhard was what so many of us will not and cannot be: a scientist who loved mankind and took a deliberate interest in its evolution. His contemporary importance derives not least from the fact that he kept his fingers on the pulse of our time and discovered new ways of accelerating it. . . . I can still picture Teilhard vividly, his finely chiselled features wearing an air of transparency, his whole figure seeming to radiate concentrated spirituality.[1]

This impression made on a man who seems to have had little sympathy with Teilhard's religious convictions may serve to sum up the purpose and the achievement of his life. If there was not to be found in his *Phenomenon* that "flat insistence" on certain theological views which seems to be required by one type of theologian, even when those views are not strictly relevant, there can be no sort of doubt of his essential orthodoxy. One needs only to glance at *Le Milieu Divin* (English translation, *The Divine Milieu*) to recognize this truth:

> It is a truly Christian duty to grow, even in the eyes of men, and to make one's talents bear fruit, even though they be natural. It is part of the essentially Catholic vision to look upon the world as maturing—not only in each individual or

[1] *Memories of Teilhard de Chardin*, p. 141.

in each nation, but in the whole human race—a specific power of knowing and loving, whose transfigured term is charity but whose roots and elemental sap lie in the discovery and the love of everything that is true and beautiful in creation. . . . The effort of mankind, even in realms inaccurately called profane, must, in the Christian life, assume the role of a holy and unifying operation.[2]

What, in fact, Teilhard has succeeded in doing, even in the sphere of technical theology, is to open up new vistas for the inspiration of the professional theologian. The following passage, unswerving in its orthodoxy, yet pregnant with fresh theological ideas, may well explain why "the theologians" were not at first able to appreciate the quality of his work. Yet it deserves not merely respect but positive enthusiasm:

In the narrow, partitioned and static Cosmos, wherein our fathers believed themselves to dwell, Christ was "lived" and loved by His followers, as He is today, as the Being on whom all things depend and in whom the Universe finds its substance. But this Christological function was not easily defended on rational grounds, at least if the attempt was made to interpret it in a full, organic sense. Accordingly Christian thinking did not especially seek to incorporate it in any precise cosmic order. At that time the Royalty of Christ could be readily expressed in terms of His ascendancy through moral law; or else it was sufficient that He should prevail in the non-experimental, extra-cosmic sphere of the supernatural. Theology, in short, did not seem to realize that *every* kind of Universe might not be compatible with the idea of an Incarnation. But with the concept of Space-Time as we have defined it, there comes into effect an harmonious and fruitful conjunction between the two spheres of rational experience and of faith. In a universe of "conical" structure Christ has a place (the apex!) ready for Him to fill, whence His spirit can radiate through all the centuries and all beings; and because of the genetic links running through all levels of Time and Space between the elements of a convergent world, the Christ-influence, far from being restricted to the mysterious zones of "grace", spreads and penetrates throughout the entire mass of Nature in movement. In such a world Christ cannot sanctify

[2] Page 79.

the Spirit without (as the Greek Fathers intuitively perceived) uplifting and saving the totality of Matter. Christ becomes truly universal to the full extent of our needs. . . .[3]

In the purely theological field then, it seems fair to claim that, far from being unorthodox, Teilhard has given to the Church a more satisfactory basis for the doctrines of the mystical body and the kingship of Christ than has any previous thinker. In the context of that *aggiornamento* desired by Pope John in the sphere of dogmatic presentation as well as in other areas of the Church's life, the work of this French Jesuit must surely be reconsidered by the traditionalists not merely with sympathy but with a genuine desire to learn. Neither the Platonism of Augustine nor the Aristotelianism of Aquinas can possibly suffice to contain the ever-developing revelation of God to man. To an age which thinks in terms unknown to either of those two great men, theologians must learn to speak a new language. That language has been provided for them by Teilhard.

It is all too easy to poke fun at his neologisms—"noosphere", "planetization" and the rest; it is possible to condemn his approach as being a mixture of mysticism and poetry; many find his optimism too facile, and suggest that he is not prepared to look the facts in the face—that he ignores the harsh realities of suffering and evil. His critics present him as a slightly comic figure, with his head in Cloud-Cuckoo-Land, muttering his strange incantations, hypnotizing himself into a belief that "all is for the best in the best of all possible worlds". A growing acquaintance with his published works ought to correct such a prejudiced attitude.

In *The Future of Man,* there are several essays which deserve special mention in this context. Thus, in an article written in Peking in February, 1942, entitled "The New Spirit", he shows himself well aware of the anguish of mankind. Without ignoring or minimizing it, he tries to relate it to his own vision of truth.

[3] *The Future of Man,* p. 94.

A great many internal and external portents (political and social upheaval, moral and religious unease) have caused us all to feel more or less confusedly, that something tremendous is at present taking place in the world. But what is it? What I wish to offer here is the outcome of my own thinking, expressed in a simple and clarified form, so that everyone may be able to understand it without ambiguity, and may criticize and (this is my great hope) correct and amplify it.[4]

One has to confess, a little wryly, that what is for him "simple and clarified" is to the average man remarkably complex and not a little obscure. But of his genuine appreciation of the world's problems, and his earnest desire to help to work out a solution there can be little doubt:

> On the one hand the overwhelming vastness of the Cosmos need no longer appal us, since the indefinite layers of Space and Time, far from being the lifeless desert in which we seemed to be lost, show themselves to be the bosom which gathers together the separate fragments of a huge Consciousness in process of growth. On the other hand, Evil in all its forms—injustice, inequality, suffering, death itself—ceases theoretically to be outrageous from the moment when, *Evolution becomes a Genesis,* the immense travail of the world displays itself as the inevitable reverse side—or better, the condition—or better still, the price, of an immense triumph. And in its turn Earth, that microscopic planet on which we are crushed together, is seen to be no longer the meaningless prison in which we thought we must suffocate; for if its limits were less narrow and impenetrable could it be the matrix in which our unity is being forged?[5]

It would be possible to quote a number of passages from the same essay to emphasize the same point that Teilhard was no idle dreamer, burying himself in a remote past and speculating about an even more remote future. He was well aware of all that was happening in the contemporary world; but he knew where his duty lay, how best he could contribute to the welfare of mankind. As he said, in a letter to his brother, written from Burma in 1938:

[4] "The New Spirit", p. 82.
[5] "The New Spirit", p. 90.

You see, then, how I am spending in the calm of ancient Nature the hours that are so full of tension for China and Europe; and you may well imagine that I am not too pleased at being a deserter. Still, I am biding my time—should it ever come—and working patiently to clarify my "message" and strengthen my platform. It seems to me more important to create a new concept of human activity than to plunge into the feverish intoxication of a political drive which already has its leaders and will never lack followers. At the same time I am watching with great anxiety the strange transmutations we are undergoing but fail to understand.[6]

What, then, is his "message"? Perhaps one short quotation from *The Future of Man* may serve as an introduction to an attempt to summarize it. An article originally published in 1946, entitled "The Spiritual Repercussions of the Atom Bomb" (and, again, the very subject indicates his concern with man's here-and-now problems) concludes with the words: "In short the final effect of the light cast by the atomic fire into the spiritual depths of the earth is to illumine within them the over-riding question of the ultimate end of Evolution, the problem of God." [7]

"The problem of God." This is what obsessed this Jesuit scientist, who could use his scientific lore to bring depth and practical significance to his religious ideas, who could find in his faith that further dimension which enriched and heightened his scientific system. It may well prove to be the case that he will become for our age what Augustine was in the twilight of the Western Empire. When Rome was sacked by Alaric the Goth, men thought that this was the end of the world. Augustine showed them that God was still the Lord of history. Today, many a man believes that science has usurped the place of religion. Teilhard lets us see that its discoveries should lead to a renewal of faith.

Ever since the regrettable story of Galileo, the Church has suffered from an entirely natural suspicion, engendered in the minds of those who put their trust in the experimental

[6] *Letters from a Traveller*, pp. 237-8.
[7] *The Future of Man*, p. 148.

method. It is possible to plead that Galileo would not have been condemned had he not ventured into the realm of theology. It is only too easy for the scientist to retort that the theologians seemed to imagine that they had some special competence in the scientific field. There is now no possibility of denying that the accident of history had linked the Church's doctrine with a scientific picture that was hopelessly out of date. We have to admit that the theologians of the seventeenth century were still thinking in thirteenth century categories.

This uneasy situation became immensely exacerbated when, in the nineteenth century, Christian theologians as a body were reluctant to accept a theory of cosmic development which was completely at variance with the traditional account of creation, based on an over-literal interpretation of the Bible. Step by step, like men fighting a rearguard action, scriptural exegetes and dogmatic theologians have gradually yielded in face of the mounting pressure of accumulating evidence in favour of the doctrine of evolution.

Today, in response to Pope John's clear-sighted recognition that the Church has gone on too long speaking a language that betrays the truth entrusted to her, because that language no longer conveys that truth to the men of this generation, the Vatican Council is at last trying to come to terms with contemporary ways of thinking. It is no exaggeration to say that, in the sphere of the physical sciences in relation to theology, no single man has done as much as Teilhard de Chardin to prepare the way for a new presentation of the immutable truth entrusted to the Church. Whereas for centuries the Church's teachers had gone on repeating the language and imagery that were appropriate to an illiterate and unscientific tribe—the breath of God rippling the waters of a primeval chaos, and the like—the geologist, the biologist, the paleontologist and the anthropologist have together developed a whole vocabulary and a world of imagery to reveal the power working from within the very fabric of the universe to produce, on a time-space scale of unimaginable vastness, the gigantic system contemplated by

the eye of the microscope and the antenna of the radio-
telescope. It was the insight and the courage of Teilhard
which not only accepted this picture but saw it as the
manifestation of that same power of God at work in his
world, more intimately and more surely than anyone had
ever realized.

There was nothing essentially novel in this picture, nothing
that had not been at least glimpsed by the mystic, hinted at
even by the Psalmist. Like a second Paul, Teilhard declared
to the modern sceptic: "What you worship but do not
know—this I now proclaim." If the theologians are prepared
to follow his lead, the Church will not merely have come to
terms with the world of science; she will have seized the
initiative.

There was a time when theology claimed the proud title
of queen of the sciences, because all departments of human
knowledge and human thinking were seen to blend together
to subserve the cause of truth, the truth of revelation coming
in to complete the findings of natural discovery. But theology
became arrogant and thought to dictate to natural reason.
And reason revolted—in the Renaissance, the Enlighten-
ment, the scientific Humanism of today. Losing sight of
the abiding truth that the incarnate Word deifies our human
activities, that the power of God is manifested in, operates
through and brings to perfection his own natural creation,
too many Christians sought to drive a wedge between the
two. Nature came to be regarded as something alien, in-
tractable, impervious to God. Alone the supernatural mat-
tered. An asceticism tinged with Manicheism joined hands
with this false supernaturalism to produce a radically false
attitude of mind towards this world of man's experience.

To enumerate all the other factors at work would take
us too far afield. But the general result was to reduce the
Church to a beleaguered force, desperately trying to salvage
as much as she could from the menacing assaults of an increasingly secularized world. It was, above all, Teilhard who
saw that God's world can never be secularized, that if it has

been left in the hands of the secularists, this is because Christians had lost something of their faith, their hope and their charity.

> We need only to look about us at the multitude of disjointed forces neutralizing each other and losing themselves in the confusion of human society—the huge realities (broad currents of love or hatred animating peoples and classes) which represents the *power of awareness* but sufficiently vast to encompass them all. We need only recall those moments in time of war when, wrested out of ourselves by the force of a collective passion, we have a sense of rising to a higher level of human existence. All these spiritual reserves, guessed at and faintly apprehended, what are they but the sure evidence that creation is still on the move, but that we are not yet capable of expressing all the natural grandeur of the human mission?
>
> Vistas such as these, I know, do not appear to come within the Christian perspective; and because of this most of those who point to them and welcome them seem at least by implication to be heralding the appearance of a religion destined to supplant all earlier creeds. But how does all this arise—the challenge on the one hand, the mistrust on the other—except out of the fact that neither we nor our adversaries have sufficiently measured the powers of growth with which Christ endowed his Church.[8]

This, again, is no essentially new idea. In his famous pastoral, *Essor ou Declin de l'Eglise,* Cardinal Suhard was asserting much the same truth:

> Messenger of Christ, the Redeemer, and instrument united with him of whom she is the living incarnation, she owes it to herself to extend to all created things the benefit of renewal. Christ did not come to excommunicate the world but to baptize it with his blood. Henceforth the Christian has not only the right but the duty to complete creation and to work in the City here below. "The temporal is a wounded reality which we must love with a redeeming love." [9]

Teilhard would perhaps question the term "wounded" as applied to temporal reality. It is indeed incomplete, because

---

[8] *The Future of Man,* pp. 21-2.
[9] Eng. translation *Growth or Decline,* Notre Dame, Ind., and London, 1948, p. 78.

still on the move, still in process of evolution. But it is an important part of man's high destiny that he should do all he can to control the onward march of the process. More and more power is being put into his hands: but also more and more responsibility:

> Hitherto Man was using matter to serve his needs. Now he has succeeded in seizing and manipulating the sources commanding the very origins of matter—springs so deep that he can release for his own purposes what seemed to be the exclusive property of the sidereal powers, and so powerful that he must think twice before committing some act which might destroy the earth. . . .
>
> Thus considered, the fact of the release of nuclear energy, overwhelming and intoxicating though it was, began to seem less tremendous. Was it not simply the first act, even a mere prelude, in a series of fantastic events which, having afforded us access to the heart of the atom, would lead us on to overthrow, one by one, the many other strongholds which science is already besieging? . . .
>
> It is thus, step by step, that Man, pursuing the flight of his growing aspirations, taught by a first success to be conscious of his power, finds himself impelled to look beyond any purely mechanical improvement of the earth surface and increase of his external riches, and to dwell upon the *growth and biological perfection of himself.* . . .
>
> So that today there exists in each of us a man whose mind has been opened to the meaning, the responsibility and the aspiration of his cosmic function in the universe. . . .[10]

This is the man to whom the Church is called upon to speak, for whose benefit she must re-interpret her age-old truth. The astonishing fact, for those whose faith needs bolstering, is that Christ's promise that the Holy Spirit would lead his followers into all truth means that, as man's vision of the universe has been enlarged, so has the Church been able to incorporate into her dogmatic system whatever aspects of that vision might be relevant to it. For the believer who is secure in the conviction that any and every truth is an expression of the abiding Truth that God is, the most

[10] *The Future of Man,* pp. 142-5.

exciting feature of any fresh discovery is that it enables him to enlarge his personal vision of God. Aware as he must be that any such vision must be woefully inadequate, he will yet feel that the majestic sweep of Teilhard's portrayal of the evolutionary process somehow deepens his awareness of the infinity and eternity of the Creator. For the Psalmist as for Pascal, for Ignatius Loyola as for Kant, the glory of God is shown forth in the silence of the starry sky. For Teilhard and for those who find inspiration in his work, the cosmos is not just an awe-inspiring spectacle; it is a world of seething energy, manifesting the power and wisdom of God.

Take, for instance, the following passage from the Old Testament and see how rich it becomes in the light of Teilhard's work:

> The Lord made me his when first he went about his work, at the birth of time, before creation began. Already I lay in the womb, when the depths were not yet in being, when no springs of water had yet broken; when I was born, the mountains had not yet sunk on their firm fountations, and there were no hills. . . . I was at his side, a master-workman, my delight increasing every day, as I made play before him all the while; made play in this world of dust, with the sons of Adam for my playfellows. . . .[11]

We are told that, three days before his death, Père Teilhard de Chardin wrote the last page of his journal—his testament to the Church and to the world. It may well serve as his epitaph:

Maundy Thursday.
What I believe.
(i) St Paul—the three verses:[12] *En pasi panta theos*
(ii) Cosmos = Cosmogenesis—Biogenesis—Noogenesis—Christogenesis
(iii) The Universe is centrated—Evolutively $\begin{smallmatrix}\text{Upward}\\\text{Forward}\end{smallmatrix}$

[11] Proverbs 8. 22-32.
[12] 1 Cor. 15. 26, 27, 28.

The two
articles of   The Christian Phenomenon
my Credo   Christ is its Centre Noogenesis = Christogenesis
                                                    (= Paul)

The last enemy to be abolished is death.

Scripture says, "He has put all things in subjection under his feet". But in saying "all things" it clearly means to exclude God who subordinates them;

And when all things are thus subject to him, then the Son himself will also be made subordinate to God who made all things subject to him, and thus God will be all in all.

CHAPTER VII

LAW, MORALS
AND RELIGION

The subject of this essay, vast in range as it is complex in ramification, is not such that one can hope to treat it with anything like completeness. Moreover, while I believe that the solution to this highly complex problem is essentially a simple one, this does not mean that it does not involve an immense subtlety of presentation, which is the obverse of dogmatic affirmation.

The subject is "topical", not alone in the sense that it has an abiding relevance to the human situation, but because, in recent years, men have sought to build a legal system divorced from morality, just as a previous generation held that morality had no essential relation to religious belief. The Kantian *Kritik,* which tried to restore the situation created by a denial of the absolute nature of Pure Reason, by replacing it with a Practical Reason which seems largely irrational was partly to blame for the earlier scepticism. Whatever the theoretical possibility of constructing a moral system without a religious basis may be, we can hardly doubt that it is no coincidence that the contemporary decline in moral standards has ensued on a widespread rejection of traditional religion. The more recent attempts to base a legal system on purely positivistic grounds, without reference to underlying moral values, is bound to impair the strength and dignity of the whole edifice of law.

Without wishing at this stage to discuss, for example, the necessity or expediency of altering the law concerning homosexual practices, it seems important to insist that this should be done only because of incidental disadvantages resulting from the existing legislation—the danger of blackmail is one obvious reason. If the distinction between "crime" and "sin" is made so absolute that men come to think that there is no essential relation between the two, then it would seem we shall be inflicting damage both on man's moral sense and on the very foundations on which the law itself rests. The moral sense will suffer because, human nature being the frail and fallible thing that it is, we all need the corrective support of some power outside ourselves to enable us to keep our feet on what is a dangerous and slippery slope. The exceptional individual, the saint or the stoic sage, may be able to do all that he should in virtue of some inner strength, without any consideration of public opinion or legal sanction. But *how* exceptional such men are.

Equally, it would seem, the law itself will increasingly fail in its effectiveness, if it is thought of as a purely man-made affair of governmental expedients. Citizens may be persuaded for a time to obey the law of the land by the argument that civilized life cannot go on without some accepted code of public behaviour; but the Augustinian maxim *Lex iniusta non est lex* finds an echo in every thinking man's heart. Legal formularies derive their significance from the recognition of a deeper foundation than the need to preserve some merely external conformity to a set of rules which clever men have arbitrarily devised.

It is surely not without significance for our present investigation that the whole corpus of law which, with whatever differences of emphasis or immediate political origin, is broadly accepted by the Anglo-Saxon and Latin nations, to say nothing of those regions of the earth which have been under their control, derives from such diverse origins. This is no place for a study in comparative jurisprudence, and what I have to say must be superficial and jejune. But we may remind ourselves of the development of Graeco-Roman law, that process of cross-fertilization by which the Romans, borrowing from the Athenians, produced by their native genius that impressive system which was one of their proudest achievements; we recall the profound intuitions of Socrates, Plato, Aristotle and the Stoics, these latter influencing the thought of Cicero, the former helping to mould the mind of Augustine. Parallel to this development, yet in origins so remote, we think of the complex system on which Judaism was nourished, that triple Law, ceremonial, judicial and moral, which survives to this day in its own right, and yet has given to the Gentile world an element which has added a new dimension to its thinking. The Justinian Code given to a Christian world by a Christian Emperor owes not less to Moses and the scribes than it does to Greek philosophy and Roman jurists. Preserved in the Catholic Church, reinterpreted by the medieval schoolmen, adapted to a different civilization by the Church's canon lawyers, all this has entered into the very life of contemporary Europe, so that it still influences the thinking of lawyers, many of whom no longer accept the foundations on which so much of it was built.

For many of these, the Law is a discipline in its own right, necessary for civilized living but intelligible by itself, without reference to the ideas which influenced those who fashioned it. Certainly one does not need to be a believer in order to be a successful practising lawyer. Certainly it is possible to discuss the nature and function of law to a considerable distance without invoking metaphysical or transcendental considerations of any kind.

We can agree that the obvious purpose of any system of law is to promote the general good. Any society or group soon finds by experience that it cannot get on without some agreed conventions, and the larger the society, the more elaborate do these conventions become. By a process of trial and error, perhaps, in other words, by purely empirical methods, man finds out for himself which rules work best. The object or purpose of the society is more easily achieved, harmony is better preserved, by this set of rules rather than that. In the larger political society which we call the state,

which has been invented by man to make life easier for everybody, by pooling resources, by employing the citizens about
tasks for which they are best suited, by banding together for
defence against common enemies, the structure becomes
highly complex and the rules or laws correspondingly intricate. But the test of a law's value remains the same: does
it help to promote the purposes of the state? Does it serve
the common good?

Yes, but what is the common good? Is it simply the production of larger and larger public buildings, bigger and more
powerful armies and so on? Are these an end in themselves,
or are they produced for the benefit of the citizens? Is there
any sense in talking about a common good, except in terms
of the good of the individuals?

When we really examine the question, we see that it is illogical, because contrary to the very purpose for which men
initially come together, to subordinate the good of the individual to that of the community. True as it is that, in detail,
the immediate advantage of the individual may have to be
sacrificed to the general good, even to the extent that the
individual may be required to lay down his life for others,
this clearly cannot be the normal requirement. For the more
the individual good was sacrificed the more would the totality
suffer; the more citizens laid down their lives, the weaker,
in the end, would the state itself become.

Therefore it follows that the true purpose of the state must
be to promote the good of the individual. What this is can be
appreciated only by an understanding of individual human
nature, the nature of man. Disregarding the extreme material-
ist view which would make man no more than a rather unfortunate animal, who, as Chesterton said "cannot sleep in
his own skin and cannot trust his own instincts", who "is a
kind of cripple, wrapped in artificial bandages called clothes
and propped on artificial crutches called furniture"—disregarding this outmoded view, we are compelled to see him as
a being who has, in fact, an attitude towards law which goes
beyond the purely pragmatic and utilitarian. While he ac-

cepts the necessity for law as a matter of practical politics, he knows, too, that the notion of obligation to obey the law is more than a matter of "doing the decent thing".

For just as he knows himself to be a creature whose needs go beyond the purely material, so he knows that, however tiresome he may find this or that law, to the extent that he does sometimes break it, he would be doing something dishonourable if he broke a law which he recognized as being reasonable. He is aware, in fact, of a *moral* obligation. This, it seems to me, is the great objection to any positivist theory of legislation. There have, as we all know, been attempts to derive the notion of moral obligation from something else, to describe its growth by a process of evolution from a state of mind which was purely non-moral, as though, from the fact that men discovered that chaos resulted when people ignored the law, it was possible to develop a sense of duty towards this purely human invention. As well suggest that an Englishman has a moral obligation to carry an umbrella on a wet day. Rather the truth seems to be that, while it is the reasonableness of a law which wins man's consent, it is this same reasonableness which lies at the root of man's sense of obligation to obey that which he has accepted.

Which brings us to the problem of the nature of moral obligation. Ever since the days of Plato's *Republic* men have argued about the meaning of justice—whether it is as Thrasymachus declared, simply the will of the stronger; whether it is a manmade convention; whether it has any absolute significance; whether indeed there is really any such thing. The interesting thing, for our immediate purpose, is that, all along, it has been the subject of debate, that men have not felt satisfied with saying: Well, there it is; you must just take it or, if you like, leave it. Their very desire to argue about it, to analyse its meaning, to *prove* it is this or that should be enough to show that it is, at any rate, not unconnected with rationality.

The attempt of the evolutionists to maintain that the consciousness of moral obligation grew out of a situation in which there was no such consciousness will not do. It is simply a form of verbal sleight-of-hand, like the patter of the conjurer who distracts your attention by talking while he is manipulating his apparatus to produce rabbits out of an apparently empty hat. We know perfectly well that, even if the rabbits were not actually in the hat all the time, they were *somewhere:* they did not just materialize out of thin air. We may not know how to do the trick; but we know enough about the nature of things to realize that the explanation involves the pre-existence of the rabbits before they actually appear. So it is with the theory that men did not originally have a sense of moral obligation, but after realizing how nasty, brutish and short life was without it, they decided to invent it. Apart from the fact that it was presumably the tougher ones who did survive, whereas, one presumes, obligation, on the theory, was invented to protect the weaker ones, no one explains how you set about inventing a mental state of which you have no sort of notion to begin with. It is all very well to beg the question by implying, as the thorough-going evolutionists do imply, that you have only to wait long enough and anything can happen. This is not an argument: it is simply a gratuitous assertion made contrary to such evidence as we do possess.

Nor again do the Utilitarians really explain why we *ought* to aim at pleasure (in however wide a sense) or to shun pain. Surely it is truer to say that I instinctively shrink from pain and seek pleasure; but I am completely unaware of any obligation to do this in my own case, nor is it easy to see how the aiming at the greatest good of the greatest number—at least in Bentham's view of good—can grow out of my personal attitude to these states. I am not denying, let me say, that we have such a duty. I am merely suggesting that the Benthamite analysis is not very helpful.

On the other hand, I must confess that I find myself in greater sympathy with Utilitarians than with Professor H. A. Prichard. While I shall always admit to having benefited enormously from listening to Prichard dissecting any philosophical statement, whether in morals or in epistemology, I never felt satisfied that he had anything better to put in place of the view he had so effectively demolished. He did a wonderfully sterilizing job in the field of moral philosophy, but I am convinced that his basic position, which owed so much to Kant, was somehow misconceived. Those of you who sat at his feet will remember the almost fanatical fervour with which he sought to isolate the notion of what was "right" or obligatory from what was "good"—in the sense of benefiting the agent in any way at all. Where he was right, I suggest, was in his assertion that to act from any motive of self-interest, however enlightened, is to destroy the peculiar quality of a moral act. Where he was wrong was in his view that not only must moral action never be thought of as benefiting the individual but that there is absolutely no reason to suppose that it will, still less that it must.

Now it is here, as it seems to me, that the traditional doctrine of a Natural Law comes to our help. To discuss it in any detail would be impossible in the space at my disposal, but very briefly this can be said. It is of the nature of things that man, if he is to prosper physically, to be healthy, to be comfortable, must take cognisance of certain truths about his environment, which the scientist would describe as laws of nature. Things are what they are and behave as they behave. Fire burns; and can be turned to good use by warming man, by cooking his food, by producing steam to drive his engines; it can also produce disastrous effects if allowed to get out of control. It is a curious and possibly significant fact that when natural forces do not act as we are accustomed to see them act, when the light does not come on as I press the switch, I may well say: "It *ought* to come on; there's something *wrong*." Now, clearly we are not using these terms in any moral sense. We are not accusing the electric plant of misbehaving morally. It is just not being normal. It is not, we might say, being itself, in the sense that it is not doing what we expect of it. We say, therefore, that there is something "wrong" with the plant. When it works, we say it is all "right".

When we apply the same terms, "right" and "wrong", to man's conduct, we are using them in a very different sense. We are passing moral judgement. And it seems to me that there is a sort of analogy between the meaning of the terms as I apply them to non-human beings and their meaning as applied to human beings. When a *man,* as we say, misbehaves, we mean that he is not behaving in a way that is characteristic of man as such. While it is regrettably true that all men not infrequently misbehave to some degree, whereas, on the whole, electric light switches do function normally, we still maintain a distinction between what is "right", that is, characteristic of man as such, and what is "wrong", that is, contrary to his true nature.

I am not referring here, of course, to conduct contrary to the laws of nature as they affect all corporeal reality. If I saw a man sail out of a window and soar gracefully into the sky, I should be surprised in the way in which I should be surprised to scc a flying pig. But were I to see a man drinking himself into a state of insensibility, I might apply the term "pig" in a way which would imply that that is the sort of thing that may be all right for pigs, but is definitely not human.

And since what is *specifically* human is the rational element in his nature, it would seem that it is here that we must look for the basis of morality. In an important and well-known passage of Cicero's *De Republica,* based as we know on Stoic teaching, we are told: "True law is right reason in agreement with nature; it is universal in application, and unchanging and eternal . . . There will not be different laws at Athens and Rome, or different laws now and in the future, but one eternal and unchangeable law will be valid for all nations and all ages." We readily accept the notion that there are certain laws of thought, logical rules, principles such as the principle of contradiction, which make it possible for men everywhere to participate in discussion. These laws control our thinking, in the sense that they enable us to reason straight, to arrive at correct conclusions, to get the right answer. We can, as we know, manipulate these laws to deceive others, by concocting false syllogisms or resorting to other fallacies. In so far as we do this deliberately, we are abusing reason. We can also fail to obey these same laws of thought, but without deliberate fault. In either case we shall be getting the *wrong* answer.

The idea of the natural law suggests that, like the laws of nature, like the laws of thought, there is a system of rational order which controls man's development, not in the sense that he is compelled to obey, but in the sense that it is through obedience to it that he will thrive and prosper, not now in the physical and material sense, not now in the strictly ratiocinative sense, but in what we have to call the moral sense. It is through reason, through an intelligent understanding of the natural forces about him that man develops his physical nature; it is through reason, through the right application of the laws of thought that he develops his understanding and his hold on truth; it is through reason, through the appreciation and conscious acceptance of this whole world of moral imperatives, that he develops his moral nature.

If all men were truly wise, they would know how to manipulate nature in such a way as to benefit from it at all times, to adapt themselves to its laws, to make full use of its resources: if all men were truly wise, their purely ratiocinative activities would be infallible; if all men were truly wise, they would always do what was morally right, because they would see the folly of acting in any other way. And further if all men were truly wise, there would be no need of human law, since the purpose of human law—the achievement of the common good through the realization of individual good—would be achieved without it.

But, since this is far from being the case, human law is needed to replace, in a sense, the natural law, to stand in for it, as it were, just as the guardian stands *in loco parentis*. The authority and functions of the guardian derive from the absent parent, and should not go beyond or fall short of the parent's wishes. So it is with the laws which man makes. Their purpose is to produce as far as possible the situation which would prevail were all men entirely reasonable and just. To quote St Thomas Aquinas: "Every law enacted by man enjoys the character of law to the extent that it is derived from the natural law."

But it would be wrong to picture the natural law as a comprehensive mass of detailed legislation, in the way in which a code of human laws is constituted of a multiplicity of enactments. It is rather like the mentality of the man of breeding and good taste, who does not need a list of instructions, a book of etiquette, describing how he ought to behave in any given situation; the book of etiquette is a substitute for the real thing. Some people object to the notion of a natural law, universal and immutable, on the grounds that, if there were such a thing, the human reflection of it would not vary so much from place to place or from age to age. But the fact is, of course, that while the natural law demands that justice be always done, what is in practice just will vary from place to place according to circumstances of every kind. Those who dislike the notion of a natural law because it seems to suggest that there is one hard and fast rule to meet every situation should ponder the words of Lord Penzance: "Law is, or ought to be, the handmaid of justice; and inflexibility, which is the most becoming robe of the latter, often serves to render the former grotesque."

> The principles of the natural law are permanent and comprehensive; but just because they are comprehensive, they have an elasticity when they come to be applied. The positive rules are variable and subject to change by human authority; but as long as they remain in force they are rigid in application. Because the principles of natural law are broad and elastic in their application, many a superficial jurist is led to deny their intrinsic immutability.[1]

[1] Wu, *Fountain of Justice*, p. 10.

Perhaps a word about "reason" in this general context may serve to remove misunderstanding. As I understand it, the reason which enables man to appreciate the natural law is not the cold mathematical ratiocinative faculty but rather what we call "nous"—which, I take it, is more comprehensive than the Greek *nous*. It is the practical reason or synderesis of Aristotle, a combination of intellect, general intelligence, experience and *savoir faire*. Any idea that the application of the natural law in the concrete is achieved by a process of logical deduction from certain major principles stated in propositional form should be rejected.

In the hope that enough has been said to bring out the nature of the link between human law, which protects and promotes those human values which are essential to live in society, and the natural law which is the very basis of all right conduct in any sphere, we may now pass on to consider the third element in our programme—religion. Forgetting for our present purposes so much that is called religion—the daily ritual, the practices of prayer and worship, the forms in which the spirit of religion is incorporated—all we need to think of is the being who is the inspirer of religion, the object of our prayers and worship. And of that being we need to isolate one attribute, that of wisdom. There is a famous passage towards the end of Aristotle's *Ethics,* in which that on the whole not particularly religious thinker, showing perhaps a rather cerebral approach to God, yet brings out the point I wish to make:

> The activity of the intellect, manifesting itself in pure specu-
> lation, is in itself pre-eminently earnest and good. Moreover
> a life thus passed will be more than human; for it will not be
> in so far as he is human that a man will lead it, but in so far
> as he has in him a divine element. . . . Since the reason is a
> divine thing if contrasted with human nature as a whole,
> the life of reason will also be divine, as contrasted with ordi-
> nary human life. . . . As far as in us lies we ought to enter
> upon our immortal heritage, by striving ever to lead a life
> conformable to that in us which is highest and best. . . . Most
> delightful, then, and of all things best for man is the life

of reason, since reason it is that constitutes the essence of human nature.

After which I should like to quote from the book of Wisdom:

> Mind-enlightening is the influence that dwells in her, set high apart; one in its source yet manifold in its operation: subtle yet easily understood . . . pure effluence of his glory who is God all-powerful, she feels no passing taint; she, the glow that radiates from eternal light, she the untarnished mirror of God's majesty, she the faithful echo of his goodness. . . . Bold is her sweep from world's end to world's end, and everywhere her gracious ordering manifests itself. . . . God of our fathers, Lord of all mercy, thou by thy word hast made all things, and thou in thy wisdom hast contrived man to rule thy creation. . . .

Again from sources so diverse we find the same essential truth. God is wisdom and man's wisdom is derived from God. What St Thomas calls the eternal law is the all-pervading rationality of the universe. At the purely scientific level, the complete agnostic recognizes this fact, which he perhaps labels the uniformity of nature. The order in the cosmos, whether or not it be ascribed, as seems most natural, to a subsistent intelligence, strongly suggests that man himself, a feature of that cosmos, is subject to that all-pervading, all-wise Love:

> That moves the sun and moon and the other stars.

Far beyond the Graeco-Roman and Hebraic civilizations, the Chinese sage Confucius perceived the same truth: "What is ordained by Heaven is essential nature. Conformity to the essential nature is called the natural law. The refinement of the natural law is called culture."

To this point then our argument seems to have reached. Man's refusal to order his life according to the principles of reason, whether stated in the specific enactments of human law or more broadly manifested in the natural law, is, to a greater or lesser extent offending against some transcendent order of reality. Manifestly, it would be ludicrous to suggest that any and every offence against the law of the land, every transgression of the Highway Code, every neglect of the municipal by-laws is a sin that cries to heaven for vengeance. But equally clearly, it is to do less than justice to the dignity of man and the significance of his actions to insist that whatever iniquity he commits is no more than an infringement of some man-made convention. The well-being of human society and the happiness of the individual would seem to require that we see in law something sacred, to be treated reasonably, in the fullest sense of that word, seen in its due relation to man's purposes here and hereafter.

No one has expressed this truth more simply and yet more sublimely than Hooker: "Of law there can be no less acknowledged than her seat is in the bosom of God, her voice the harmony of the world; all things in heaven and earth do her homage, the very least as feeling her care, and the greatest as not exempted from her power."

We may well feel that, at this stage, the whole thesis I am propounding has left the earth and taken off for the empyrean. Well, I was not proposing to write a handbook for lawyers and magistrates, to help them in the administration of the law. My aim has been rather to sketch out an ideal philosophy of law, to see a vision of the City of God, that unrealized Utopia, which yet serves, like Plato's *Republic,* to teach certain important practical truths. The mere term "City of God" has become so identified with that rather ferocious Christian, Augustine, that many people are put off by it. The sense in which I should like to apply it to our present theme is that of a society, ruled by the perfect wisdom which is, in fact, the pursuit of all men, whatever their religious beliefs. Religion, of course, adds colour, depth, richness to what might otherwise be a somewhat arid view of reality; but the quest for truth, with its implication of subsistent wisdom, is the all but universal concern of mankind. Behind the ever-changing phenomena marches, rank on rank, "The army of unalterable law".

What men need to appreciate is the idea that the natural law, submission to which is the secret of man's success, is not the capricious invention of some unpredictable being, but is the expression of an eternally valid system of truth, beyond the range of man's comprehension yet ever the object of his pursuit. All men are content to accept the notion that the material universe is subject to law; it is a curious quirk of our nature that we cannot admit an analogous truth concerning the moral law. Yet, to quote Confucius again (lest we seem to be arguing solely from Christian or Jewish beliefs): "These moral laws form the same system with the laws by which the seasons succeed each other and the sun and moon appear with the alternations of day and night."

To sum up then: Human law is valid in so far as it is a specification, an application to the concrete situation, of the natural law, which is the law of man's well-being. The natural law, in its turn, is the application to man of the eternal law by which God rules the universe, that product of his wisdom and his power. It is possible, as we know, to consider human law in isolation from the natural law, just as it is possible, at least in theory, to accept a general moral system, applicable to mankind as a whole, without reference to God. But, as it would seem, the most comprehensive and most intellectually satisfying view is that which I have tried to sketch. In the knowledge and love and worship of God, man finds his fulfilment; and an important, indeed essential, part of that worship would seem to be the service and love of our fellow-men, involving duties based upon our common nature and expressed in principle in the natural law, in practice in human law, resting upon and specifying that same natural law. Law, morals and religion are three levels of one fundamental reality.

CHAPTER VIII

TRUTH IN ST AUGUSTINE

There are, it would seem, two lines of approach to the general problem of truth—two attitudes which may roughly be described as *minimal* and *maximal*.

The minimal attitude is that of a Descartes who, obsessed as it were with the fact of error, with the fact that we are constantly making mistakes in detail, asks himself whether perhaps the whole process of what we call *knowing* isn't itself a gigantic error, whether I can in fact *know*, in the fullest sense of that word, anything at all. Descartes, as everybody knows, snapped out of this neurotic condition by deciding that even the very process of doubting everything necessarily implied the existence of a doubter. The doubter himself existed prior to his doubts. *Cogito ergo sum.*

But the bother is that this minimal, negative attitude has bedevilled much philosophical speculation ever since. If, when you think at all, you are constantly looking over your shoulder, as it were, you are liable to develop a permanent crick in the neck which is not conducive to seeing straight. It is for this reason, among others, that I have chosen to write on the subject of *Truth* in St Augustine. There are few thinkers, I believe, with a more robust and healthy approach to the whole topic of human thinking and, however unpopular such an approach may be, I am sure that it is one which needs constant re-examination and reassertion.

Not that Augustine himself was always entirely untroubled by the sceptical challenge. We know from his writings that he was for a time attracted by the negative and destructive criticism of the New Academy. "When I was in Italy, I often held converse with myself as to the way in which Truth is to be found . . . often it seemed to me that there was no finding of it, and the tide of my thinking set strongly towards the position of the Academics." [1]

What was that position? It was not the out and out scepticism which denies the possibility of any knowledge; but it did suggest that absolute certainty is unattainable and that, in practice, we must remain content with a greater or less degree of probability. We need not dwell on Augustine's theory that the Academics didn't really believe in their disbelief, but used it as a pedagogic method to scare off those who weren't likely to be serious philosophers, so that only the tough-minded and mentally energetic need apply. In his later writings he felt it necessary to use all the weapons in his armoury against what he clearly regarded as a dangerous attitude. In one of his letters he says that if it gets about that acute philosophers believe that truth is indiscernible, men in general would settle down into a lethargic condition from which even the last trump would hardly arouse them.

He therefore develops an argument very similar to the Cartesian *cogito*. Sensations do indeed lead to erroneous judgements of every sort: he instances the hackneyed case of the oar in the water looking bent, and the way in which towers seem to move as we sail past them. But the conviction that I am alive is a conviction unshakable by any sceptical insinuation. "Let then a thousand kinds of deceptive objects of vision be presented to a man who says—I know I am alive: he won't be afraid of them because even if he is deceived he is *alive*." Moreover, "everyone who knows that he is in doubt about something knows a truth, and in regard to this he knows that he is certain—therefore, he is certain about a truth: consequently, everyone who doubts if there be a truth has in himself a true theory in which he does not doubt. Con-

---

[1] Cf. John of Salisbury, *Metalogicon*, "he himself holds the Academic position that there are some matters about which the wise man may permit himself to doubt".

sequently, whoever for whatever reason can doubt, ought not to doubt that there is truth."

Now all this is no more than a rather obvious piece of dialectic. I have dwelt on it a little, not because it is particularly characteristic of Augustine, still less because it provides the basis of his general position, but as a guarantee that Augustine is not unaware of the problem raised by the fact of hallucination, or indeed of the many difficulties involved in the whole question of sense-perception.

But while sense-experience does, as we know, lead to error, it is nevertheless important that we recognize the role of imagination in the process of human knowledge.

> Owing to that very order of our nature whereby we are made mortal and carnal, we handle visible things more easily and with a greater sense of familiarity than intelligible things. . . . Our familiarity with bodies is so great and our thought has projected itself outward with so wonderful a proclivity towards them that, after withdrawing from the uncertainty which is characteristic of material things, to fix itself to a much more certain and fixed knowledge on that which is spirit, it yet flies back to those bodies and settles down in that place whence it drew its very weakness. We must accommodate ourselves to this feebleness, so that whenever we try to distinguish more suitably and investigate more directly interior spiritual realities, we must take illustrative examples from exterior corporeal realities.[2]

Now that passage is, I admit, a bit too Platonic for the modern palate and I have no doubt that if Augustine had read *Concept of Mind* he would have phrased things a bit more carefully. But it does surely make it clear that Augustine is a man after Professor Ryle's own heart. He is, it is true, a bit too slick in distinguishing between interior and exterior, spiritual and corporeal: but an acquaintance with Augustine's history as well as a reading of his works makes it quite certain that, in approaching the subject of Truth, Augustine was not likely to disregard the contribution made by sense-experience. On the contrary, it is the sceptic, not the believer,

[2] *De Trinitate,* xi, i, i.

who belittles the contribution of sense-experience to knowledge.

> Whereas there are two kinds of knowable things—one, of
> those things which the mind perceives by the bodily senses,
> the other of those which it perceives by itself—these philoso-
> phers (namely, the Academics) have battled much against the
> bodily senses but have never been able to throw doubt upon
> these absolutely certain perceptions of things true, which the
> mind knows by itself, such as is that which I have mentioned,
> "the knowledge that I am alive". But far from us to doubt the
> truth of what we have learned by the bodily senses: since
> by them we have learned to know heaven and earth . . . far
> be it from us too to deny that we know what we have learnt
> from the testimony of others, otherwise we don't know that
> there is an Atlantic Ocean; we don't know of the existence and
> performances of men of whom we learn by reading history;
> we don't know where we were born or who our parents are;
> since on all these things we have accepted the testimony of
> others. So we have to admit that not only our own senses but
> those of other persons also have added very much indeed to
> our knowledge.

I have quoted this passage at some length because it is
important for us to bear in mind that Augustine thinks of
the process of arriving at truth as one involving the whole
person. At the same time he would cordially agree with
Professor Ryle that "having a sensation is not an exercise
of a quality of intellect or character". For him the attainment
of truth, *knowing, is* the exercise of qualities of both intellect
and character. It is this idea, I think, which lies at the back
of Augustine's famous dictum: *Crede ut intellegas*—"believe
as a means to understanding".

What I have said hitherto is largely introductory. There is
a real danger of our thinking of Augustine as completely
unrealistic in his approach to philosophical problems—unrealistic, I mean, in the sense that his theories are thought
not to be rooted in experience but are the fruit of some
a priori doctrinaire attitude, based on a flight from sense and
even from reason. Nothing could be more mistaken. Even
when the soul of Augustine takes flight and soars into the

empyrean, his whole argument invariably starts from some concrete illustration or some personal experience. In a famous passage at the end of Conf. VII, this sentence occurs: "As I sought how it came about that I admired physical beauty, whether in the heavens or the earth, and could form sound judgements about changing objects, saying 'this is as it should be, but not that', I had come upon the changeless and veritable eternity of truth beyond my changing mind . . . *inveneram incommutabilem et veram veritatis aeternitatem supra mentem meam commutabilem.*"

In other words, the very capacity to appreciate beauty, the very ability to pass aesthetic or moral judgements imply a standard of appreciation, a criterion of judgement. What is this standard and where and how is it to be found? Employing language derived to a great extent from Plato and Plotinus, Augustine fell back on the theory of an intelligible world, constituted somehow of *intelligibilia*—concepts or ideas which are, to the mind, what physical objects are to the sense-organ. The individual, soul-indwelt body, is a portion of a world which is spirit-indwelt matter. I can think of my body in terms of physical and chemical components: as such it is akin to the physicochemical compound which is the matter about "me". But I am not just physical and chemical compound in uneasy alliance with some mysterious power called soul or spirit: soul is the very spirit of unity and co-ordination, turning the multiplicity of matter into a single reality—*myself*.

I am then this dual being—capable of feeling, and in and through feeling coming to a certain inchoate knowing. But feeling and the corresponding *knowing* is an unstable and fluid business: only at the level of intellectual awareness do I arrive at changeless and certain knowledge, a knowledge in virtue of which I enter into some relationship with an abiding and changeless world.

What is that relationship? Augustine insists that to think of it in terms of purely rational "cognitive" activities is to restrict and impoverish it and, in the end, to falsify it. Once again, surprising as it may seem, Augustine would welcome Professor Ryle's attack on the view that the Mind "is in some important sense tripartite, that is that there are just three ultimate classes of mental processes". For, in the end, Augustine asserts you can only *know* the truth by *loving* it.

In other words, the relationship existing between my mind and the world of changeless truth is not a relationship that can be described as purely *cognitive;* for all his intellectual vocabulary, I doubt very much whether Augustine would have regarded that relationship as *primarily* cognitive.

For Augustine the fundamental human experience is that of *loving* rather than *knowing*. His own history was one of growth and development in love and while, both as student and as a teacher of rhetoric, he had pursued the life of an intellectual, we know all too well that he was what he was, in virtue of the nature and object of his *love*. He was aware, too, that it was love which controlled his vision, even while that vision, to some extent, affected his love. But certainly, if he was to attempt to state his deepest convictions about ultimate reality, it was inconceivable that he should do it solely in terms of cold reason.

It is indeed possible to advance some rational arguments, to prepare the soul as it were for the full revelation of the truth, to bring the unbeliever to the threshold, to give some hint of the full glory. But anyone who has studied Augustine's arguments for, say, the existence of God will surely see that he is not attempting to convince the sceptic so much as to relate man's intellectual processes to the large pattern of reality as a whole. You are, he seems to imply, an intelligent being—not just that, but that among other things. The world is a place in which you find yourself at home in different ways—and not least because it is intelligible. It is much more than that, but the experience you have of it in other ways is something private and incommunicable: however much I may talk to you about our different kinds of awareness, in the end we cannot swap them, or share them. All we can do is to talk about them: in intelligent converse we can effect a meeting. If what I say to you makes sense to you, and *vice versa,* that can only be because of a common language and a common stock of ideas. Not that ideas are like buns that we divide. In all this business we realize that pictorial language is used non-pictorially—just as the letters and figures I write on a cheque make that piece of paper so much more valuable than it is *in itself.* In order to explain how that comes about, I should have to give you a lesson in the economics of banking. I should also have to prove to you somehow that I have got some money in the bank: and my explanation would involve incursions into psychology and social behaviour and perhaps ethics.

But there isn't any time for all that: and in the case of normally educated people it isn't necessary. So is it with much of the language we use: its superficial sense may seem crude and material, so that a clever dialectician might try to make us waste a lot of time in "justifying" our use of it. But human thinking goes on despite the dialectician: just as banking goes on, however odd a process it may seem to the uninitiated.

Well then, unity, symmetry, proportion are facts which we can discuss: clearly they are not grasped by the organs of sense, for they don't possess the qualities of colour or smell or taste which mediate sense-awareness.

> I have, it is true, seen very fine lines—fine as a spider's web— drawn by architects: but there is a great difference between them and the lines which the mind thinks of: they are not images of the lines which my bodily eye told me about: they are known by anybody who is aware of them within, apart from any thought of material reality. Similarly the numbers we use for counting are different from and are not images of the groups of things which we count—groups which are grasped by the bodily senses.

All this, I know, raises tricky problems and Augustine is, perhaps, rather too blandly assuming much that many would like to argue about. But elsewhere he comes more closely to grips with the sceptic. "We admit (he says) that we are superior to animals in the possession of reason: we admit the reality of what we see with physical sight, but some animals see better than we do: are we then to refuse to admit the reality of what our senses see?"

Surely the opposite is true: the laws of number are permanent and unchanging: specific numbers of things are meaningful only in so far as they are subsumed under them.

A brief summary of Augustine's argument at this stage may be worth giving: Truth is something discovered by man, not created by him: to it and its laws man's mind is subject. For man's mind is a changeable thing; truth is eternal and immutable: it is in fact, if not synonymous with God, something belonging to him.

But at this stage, I think, Augustine would claim that reason of itself is worthless. "Understanding is faith's reward: do not then seek to understand so that you may have faith: have faith so that you may understand: *Crede ut intellegas.* . . . If we wished first to know and then to believe, we should not be able either to know or to believe."

Then we come to a dead end? Are we driven to the conclusion that, since our efforts at understanding cannot take us all the way, that indeed they are bound to fail without faith, we should give up trying to understand and wait for faith to come along? Hardly. Augustine is himself insistent that we should set great store by the intellect. *Intellectum valde ama*—he writes in one of his letters. "Far from us the thought that God hates that in which he has made us superior to other animals: far from us an assent of sheer faith which should dispense us from accepting or needing reason." Faith does not exclude reason: wisdom cannot exclude faith.

Where, then, do we go from here? Well, let us remind ourselves that, for Augustine, the pursuit of truth is equated with the pursuit of happiness. That is to say, it is not a departmental, professional activity, isolated and divorced from my whole personal development. Let me by all means conscientiously follow my intellect wherever it may lead me: but let me not suppose that it will lead me all the way. And it will lead me aright only if I accept its limitations. We have to remember that we begin our education under authority. "The natural order is that authority precede reason when we wish to learn anything": the child learns from parents, the schoolboy from his master. We use our reason, of course, to scrutinize, criticize, it may be to reject what we are taught—but not wantonly, not from a mere desire to be independent, different, superior. And if in all branches of knowledge docility and a decent humility are essential, will they not be supremely necessary in the search for wisdom and complete happiness?

Augustine, then, draws a picture of final Truth as he sees it—a world of transcendent beauty, of which the beauty we know and desire is but a faint and fading reflection: a world of absolute truth, at which our fumbling and faltering knowledge is but a feeble guess: a world of perfect happiness, in which all our desires will be richly satisfied, our disappointments and failures wholly compensated. In our present experience, we know that the happy man is not the philosopher in his study, the hedonist in his luxury flat, the aesthete in his ivory tower: these are but partially satisfied—as indeed are all men in this uncertain and perilous existence. "What soul, then, hungering for eternity and shocked by the shortness of this present life would resist the splendour and the majesty of the authority of God?"

Faith? or credulity? To the believer there can be no doubt—to the unbeliever Augustine can only say, "For the present, my aim in dealing with you must not be to make you understand—for that you cannot do—but to excite in you some desire to understand". Desire and knowing go hand in hand with wisdom. Augustine's hope is that the genuine seeker after truth, having glimpsed truth itself, will pursue it with simple-minded desire. As he writes to Consentius: "Talent enough is yours to think out your thought: but, what is more, you are upright and humble enough to desire to know what is true."

Now I admit that much of this language will seem to be crying out for radical therapeutic treatment. I realize that to much of it the label "emotive" will be firmly tied and it will be thrown into the large waste-paper basket which the analyst keeps conveniently to hand. But a label is not necessarily a death-warrant. There are whole realms of experience—personal relationships of various kinds, literary and artistic activities, most, in fact, of what gives us happiness in life—which fortunately are beyond the reach of the analyst. Life is much more than a matter of tying granny-knots (or reef knots), of feeling sick or looking pale, of thrills, twinges, pangs, throbs, wrenches, itches, prickings, chills, glows, loads, qualms, hankerings, curdlings, sinkings, tensions, gnawings and shocks. Professor Ryle can say that a man's "politeness is merely his inclination to pass the salt when it is wanted, as well as to perform a thousand other courtesies of the same general kind". But we all know that our thought about him is not that he is "salt-passing-sort-of-man". A woman is grateful to a man for his love of her, not because it is "merely his inclination to give her all that he can in the way of presents and so on": she knows that the very presents are symbolic of some permanent underlying attitude of him, as a person, to herself, as a person. So, finally, what Augustine would call his love of God is much more than his inclination to act in this or that way, to be unselfish on all occasions, to be industrious, to be sober. It is, again, a permanent fact, emerging into consciousness from time to time; it indicates the kind of person he is and not just the kind of way in which he behaves.

Let me then try to sum up the conclusions of this chapter. Augustine starts, as we all must, with the empirical facts of everyday awareness. He admits that, at this level, our knowledge is a kaleidoscopic and varying thing, with any number of mistakes in detail, though resulting in a general body of tolerably accurate information. But that is not the most important point of the story. We do not owe it to any sensation that we make a distinction between right and wrong, nor can that distinction be explained or described in terms of language derived from sensation; similarly, the force of a logic argument is not sense-derived. He would claim, then, that there must somehow exist a body of intellectual "facts"— laws of thought, moral principles and so forth—which control and condition my thinking more precisely than bodies affect my sense-organs.

By what is admittedly a metaphor, he holds that we *see* intellectual truth—we *see* that $7 + 3 = 10$, we *see* that a valid syllogism concludes, we see that change implies a changeless standard of measurement—just as we *see* birds and ships and towers. For both activities we need light, we cannot see in the dark.

It is at this stage that Augustine, following Plato, yet makes a huge advance on him. The intellectual activity of which all men are capable brings them to the recognition of the existence of a higher order of reality than the purely material. But for the full recognition of what that order is, he demands faith. It is, in the end, God who is the supremely real and the supremely intelligible. But, just as the human eye cannot gaze directly upon the sun which is the source of all light, and therefore the condition of all vision, so the human mind cannot *see* the reality that is God, albeit he is the source of all that is, and therefore the condition of all knowledge.

Yet it is only in the light, which he is, that we come to see and know whatever we grasp of intellectual or moral truth. The fullness of truth, truth without alloy or imperfection, *is* God; whatever of fragmentary truth we come to know, we know in the light he gives to enable us to *see*. *Dominus illuminatio mea.*

PART III

THE CHRISTIAN AS EDUCATOR

CHAPTER IX

ST THOMAS AND EDUCATIONAL THEORY

The history of human progress—in so far as there is such a thing—may be described as the result of the interaction of the forces of Conservatism and Innovation. The interaction is, unfortunately, rarely achieved in a wholly rational way, or in a way that does not cause chaos and disorder in a greater or less degree. In the individual there is present a love of the familiar and the conventional, manifesting itself in the attachment to the favourite arm-chair, the routine of daily habit, the dislike of the unfamiliar; but this quality may easily grow into a vice, and we have all known men and women who seem to have lost all their individuality in the acceptance of purely conventional values and an almost automatic performance of a round of unvarying tasks. For change is a law of life; since life, in our experience, manifests itself in growth. And while we like to find our friends the same, we should think them incomplete if they remained literally the same, showing no desire for development, no ambition, no interest in discovery. And the pioneer, the explorer, the inventor, have always held a high place in man's esteem. But again the desire for novelty can easily become a vice; the desire for change degenerate into mere instability; the quest of the unknown be little more than a flight from oneself and traditional values.

On a larger scale the same dangers beset men in the world of politics and economics, of literature and philosophy. It might well be argued that the last war was but the outcome of the tension set up between an excessive conservatism, a contentment with the *status quo* simply as such, and an explosive exaggeration of the claims of revolutionary change. In such a situation it is not always easy to keep one's head. The danger is lest we should either fall back upon an almost instinctive reaction or surrender to the demand for violent change without examining the nature of the change suggested.

Now it is against this sort of background that we must study the whole question of educational reform. No one will deny that the ferment existing in present-day educational theory is, in itself, a phenomenon to be welcomed. In spite of all the cranks who have entered the field of educational activity, in spite of all the "modern" schools and pedagogical "stunts' which are a feature of the age, none but the most hidebound reactionary will refuse to admit that there is any amount of need for change and development in the planning and practice of this all-important matter. But the pity is that, while authority is much concerned with problems of administration and experts are for ever discussing method and technique, it is not clear that anyone is giving sufficient thought to the underlying principles of "learning", to the nature and quality of the human mind, to the individual's capacity for assimilating knowledge, to the conditions under which the student's teachableness may be best made use of.

At the same time, of course, we may take some comfort from the undoubted fact that, in this sphere as in so many others, nature comes in to supply for the defects and to correct the errors of the misguided or freakish or sluggish pedagogue. In the end, in spite of all planners and theorists, children do continue to be educated: some of them—"by some divine chance"—very well indeed. But, among the mass of even the "educated classes", what a wastage there is! And of the semi-educated, how little do the majority seem to have profited from their years of schooling! It may be that, in attempting anything like universal education, men are trying to achieve the impossible. It may be that we must always remain content to have an educated few thinking for the many. But so long as we are committed to planning for the education of the many, it is only sensible that we should try to think the whole problem out from first principles, and not rest content to let matters drift. And, as we have implied, such a thinking out of the problem will consist in some harmonizing of "new" discoveries with a traditional body of principles, thought out by men who have no special axe to grind.

It is therefore surely a matter for congratulation that St Thomas has given us a treatise on education. For, if we are enabled to understand our educational problems in the light of the *philosophia perennis,* we shall have some confidence that our solution will be in accordance with the needs of man's nature, as analysed for us by the master. And if ever there was a time when serious thinking about education was demanded it is now. Few will dispute the statement that one of the major problems to be faced today is that of restoring Christian values to a generation seeking a safeguard against a repetition of the insane violence of war. Many will hope to find it in economic planning or political system-making. We know that it can only be found in a healthy philosophy, clearly seen and accepted as widely as may be. And that means rearing a generation of Christian-minded men.

This chapter, then, is based largely on the *De Magistro* of St Thomas, a treatise to be found among the *Quaestiones De Veritate.* The question is divided into four articles dealing with these topics:

    i. Can teaching be given by one man to another; or is God the only teacher?
    ii. Can a man be his own teacher?
    iii. Can a man be taught by an Angel?
    iv. Does teaching belong to the active or to the contemplative life?

The average person who is acquainted with modern education speculation will find something almost unreal about the very wording of the subjects to be discussed. It will be seen that there is no question of elaborating a syllabus, of weighing the respective merits of Herbart and Mme Montessori, of the Dalton Plan and its variations, of the Classical curriculum and the technical school. And some of us may find that a relief. It is not proposed, therefore, to produce from the teaching of St Thomas a fully fledged syllabus of Christian education, as one might behold Minerva springing fully armed from the head of Jupiter. Nor shall we seek to prove that whatever is of value in modern educational theory —from Pestalozzi to Dewey—is to be found in the pages of the *De Magistro*. The "accidentals" of education vary enormously from age to age and from country to country. For the moment we are not interested in the accidentals.

At the same time, lest we should be put off by plunging straight into the Thomist analysis, it may be profitable if we try to work out for ourselves some principles concerning the process which we describe as education. We have all had some acquaintance with that process; and we must all have formed some impressions concerning it. Now I take it that we should all unhesitatingly answer "Yes" to the question: "Can one man teach another?" Thus whenever we tune in to the news, we do so in order to learn something. We should hardly describe the process of listening to a radio newscommentator as constituting education in the full sense of the word. But even that is *part* of our education. For, while we stress the importance of character-training and the like, we do seem to have a prejudice in favour of the idea that education consists primarily in the transference or imparting of information. A well-educated person is one who, at the least, is well informed on a variety of topics. So this problem of the acquisition of knowledge may provide the starting-point for our investigation.

What happens when a child learns the multiplication table or the parts of an irregular verb? Through eye or ear he receives certain impressions, certain symbolic sights or sounds, which in that mysterious alembic which we call the mind are transmuted into "knowledge". Now, what is the teacher's part in this process? First and foremost, of course, it consists in the presentation of the symbols: and some teachers seem to suppose that their function stops there; that when they have made the unfortunate child "learn lists" of irregular verbs or lists of dates or the rivers of South America, they have somehow succeeded in furthering the child's education. In other words, for them teaching is a form of animal training; and we have the expression "parrot-wise" to condemn such a notion.

This characteristic is at the basis of two of the difficulties which St Thomas proposes against the suggestion that teaching of one man by another is possible at all. "If a man does teach," he argues, "it will only be through symbols (*signa*). But the mere proposing of symbols does not convey knowledge. For example, if I am trying to explain what walking is, it is no use just walking: because there will be more elements than one in my 'symbol'. And unless the pupil knows which precise element I am illustrating, he will fail to grasp the point of the demonstration. Besides, if I propose a symbol, either the pupil knows the thing symbolized or he does not. If he knows it already, there is no point in my demonstration; if he does not, then the precise meaning of the symbol must elude him, because he does not know the thing symbolized. For example, the pupil will learn nothing from the name 'rock', if he does not already know what a rock is."

Now anyone with any real experience of teaching will realize the force in these objections. And if we do appreciate the difficulty, we shall begin to understand why so much of the time we spend in "teaching" does not seem to produce any commensurate effect in our pupils. This failure is perhaps most conspicuous in the teaching of languages. For here we have to do with a double set of symbols so to speak. The English word "not", for example, is a symbol expressing the idea of negation in more than one context. Now, until the pupil has begun to appreciate the shades of meaning symbolized by that one word, he will obviously be at sea when he discovers that there are two or three symbols in another language to express the different ideas which are "symbolized" by one word in English. *He is not doing this* becomes in Latin *Hoc NON facit,* but *Do not do this* becomes *NE hoc feceris.* Inevitably the pupil thinks that the "foreigner" has an odd sort of mind, or is just being arbitrary; he has failed to realize that the English symbol stands for different shades of meaning.

Again, teachers who have experimented with the Direct Method soon realize how very carefully and exactly symbols have to be selected and proposed if there is to be any intelligent response on the part of pupils. For instance, if I want to teach a class the French for aeroplane, and I produce a picture of a Spitfire, I can hardly blame the modern youth if he goes away with the idea that *avion* is the French for Spitfire and not for *any* type of heavier-than-air machine.

It can be seen, then, that St Thomas's objections are more than captious. They are based on a real appreciation of human psychology. Again, there is real point in his assertion that, since it is the *intellect* that knows, and teaching can only be by means of *sensible* symbols, teaching as it is ordinarily understood must be ineffective for the production of true knowledge. And further, that certitude which is necessary for genuine knowledge cannot arise *directly* from sensible symbols. To elucidate this, let us return to our Spitfire illustration. Obviously, even if I do succeed in teaching my pupil that the French for aeroplane is *avion,* I cannot seriously maintain that the pupil possesses this knowledge simply as the result of my presenting to his gaze a two-dimensional picture, a silhouette, of a three-dimensional object. Into the activity which results in the possession of that knowledge has gone how much previous experience, inference, interpretation, and the like. How is the teacher to control and direct this activity, to preclude misinterpretation and ensure accuracy?

It would clearly be possible to prolong this analysis almost indefinitely but, while I believe that this would be highly profitable, I fear that some of my readers may feel that I am labouring the obvious, and that all these theoretical difficulties *solvuntur ambulando.* I will therefore refrain from further elaboration: merely remarking that, while it is true that in spite of all these alleged difficulties, boys and girls continue to acquire knowledge that is both accurate and certain by means of precisely such sensible pictures, I believe that the successful teacher is the individual who, consciously or not, is aware of the enormous mass of interpretation and inference that goes on in the pupil's mind: and that, in the end, the more important part of the activity known as "education" is that which occurs in the mind of the pupil: in a word, that our emphasis should be much more on *learning* than on teaching. In fact, before passing on to consider St Thomas's own positive contribution to the psychology of learning, we may profitably reflect on the objection which he bases on a passage of Boethius: "Through teaching, the mind of man is only stimulated to know. But he who stimulates the intellect of another to know does not make it know, any more than he who stimulates another to seeing with his eye makes him see."

St Thomas's theory of education is based upon the doctrine of forms. In his view, education is possible because the individual possesses the potentiality of all knowledge. But such potentiality is no mere passive potentiality. That is to say, the mind of man is not like a block of marble, passively submitting to be shaped into this or that statue—an Apollo, a Rima or a Thinker—simply in accordance with the activity of the sculptor and his chisel. Now this is an important point. For while the unsuccessful teacher readily blames the pupil for his failure, we are liable to fall into the mistake of supposing that the mind of the child is like a blank sheet of paper upon which the good teacher can produce this or that design, this or that pattern of knowledge, according to the demands of parents and the requirements of the Examinations Board. No, insists St Thomas. The child's potentiality for knowledge is an *active* potentiality. To illustrate this, he instances the case of medical treatment. Health is brought about in a patient primarily through the efficacy of nature in him. St Thomas would subscribe to the sentiment which, I understand, is set up in a certain Medical School clubroom in

Boston: "We dress the wound, God heals it." It is the active reaction of the patient's constitution to the doctor's treatment which produces the cure. Similarly, it is the pupil's active reaction to the teacher's instruction which produces knowledge. To quote St Thomas's own words:

> When something exists in active complete potentiality, the extrinsic agent acts only by helping the intrinsic agent and by ministering to it those things by means of which it comes forth into actuality . . . just as a doctor in healing is a minister to nature which does the principal work—ministering by abetting nature and by applying the medicines which nature uses as instruments for healing. . . . Hence, one man is said to teach another because the teacher proposes to another, by means of symbols, the discursive process which he himself goes through by natural reason, and thus the natural reason of the pupil comes to a cognition of the unknown through the help of what is proposed to him. . . . As then a doctor is said to cause health in a sick person through the operation of nature, so a man is said to cause knowledge in another through the operation of the learner's natural reason—and this is to teach.

It follows, then, from this analysis by St Thomas that, in spite of the teacher's natural prejudice, the really fruitful activity in the complex process which we call education must come from the side of the learner. It is therefore the teacher's responsibility to produce the conditions under which that activity will best be stimulated. St Thomas does not discuss the important problem in so many words, but his whole technique gives us a clue as to his mind on the subject. Modern educational theory insists much on the paramount importance of interest. The child will only *learn* if the desire to learn, the *interest* in learning, is present. And the great practical problem of the educator is how to produce this attitude of *interest* or *expectancy*. Now men are coming to see more and more that this will normally be produced where the child is conscious of a problem. Wise men realize that the ideal pupil is not one whose mind is a featureless blank, but one who has a question to ask. Unfortunately, the conditions of modern education, with its pursuit of examination-results, preclude the possibility of stimulating an interest in the raising and solving of problems. Educational mass-production inevitably means the rubber-stamp method. Cram-books, cyclostyled sheets, and "model answers" are, from the point of view of genuine education, on a par with the whip and red-hot iron of the animal-tamer.

Consider, by contrast, the technique employed by St Thomas himself. (It is to be admitted that he is dealing with adult education; but his methods apply, *mutatis mutandis,* to education at other levels.) First of all, then, he ensures that the learner shall be conscious of a problem. (Many a teacher will perhaps think him unduly optimistic in accepting the Aristotelian dictum that "all men have a natural desire to learn"! But possibly the conspicuous absence of this hunger and thirst after knowledge in so many of the occupants of modern classrooms is to be attributed to an early thwarting of it by misguided teachers.) And it is to be noted that St Thomas is not content merely to state the problem and then give the answer. His method of proposing objection after objection is entirely sound, according to the best pedagogical theory. Anyone who has spent some time in the study of his works knows how the method of presenting objections first— even though some of them are obviously specious and at times futile—has the effect of stimulating interest in the dis-cussion embodied in the *corpus articuli.*

So we may be sure that he would suggest that the most effective pedagogical method would be one which, beginning with the undoubted state of questioning about the nature of his environment, possessed by every normal child, would go on to construct a system of discovery in which the solution of one problem leads on to the realization of a further one lying behind that solution, and so on. For his whole theory of the "active potentiality" of the human mind for knowledge implies a belief that the actualization of such a potentiality is an entirely natural and spontaneous process, which only re-quires the stimulus of the appropriate environment—namely, of the fitting pedagogical method—to ensure its continuous and harmonious development. But this, of course, means that a successful education will only be achieved when it is planned as a whole, and with emphasis all the time on the nature of the developing mind, and not, as at present, in accordance with an unscientifically devised curriculum of *subjects,* an uncoordinated mass of knowledge which is thought to be necessary for "practical life" after the school age.

It follows from all this that the only successful educator will be the man or woman who has made it his or her business to approach the whole subject from the angle of the child— one, too, who appreciates the teleology of human existence. Since education is not the imposition of a form on an indifferent object, but is no more than the presentation of the ideal conditions in which the self-active agency of the human mind may be enabled to *develop itself* in accordance with its own inherent tendencies, it is manifest that from failure to understand those tendencies can only result a thwarting or perverting of them. At the same time, of course, it would be false to experience and merely insincere to suggest that only a specifically religious background will produce a humane education, whether in the intellectual or the moral sphere. For while it is undoubtedly true that, in Tertullian's words, the human soul is, of its nature, made for Christianity, it is none the less certain that all its natural powers can be developed without any explicit recognition of Christian truth. They who would argue otherwise do no service either to education or to Christianity.

Certainly St Thomas would give no support to such an argument. The psychological and metaphysical scheme which lies at the basis of his educational theory demands the recognition of the First Cause, which we call God. But we might well substitute "Nature" for "God" without doing violence to the coherence of the doctrine. For Nature is, after all, but the medium through which God works. As St Thomas reminds us in a sentence combining metaphysical truth with a profound spiritual insight: "The First Cause, from the abundance of its goodness, confers upon other things, not only that they

should be, but also that they should be causes." It is therefore surely to be expected that a purely natural education
should be entirely possible, even as, to extend the application
of St Thomas's own medical analogy, a doctor may be wholly
competent in his own sphere without possessing any religious
convictions whatsoever.

Yet it remains true that education is never complete, that
the earlier stages of intellectual and moral development which
coincide roughly with the years of schooling are only a
preparation for that fuller life of action, which is the medium
in and through which man grows up as a responsible rational
agent. And in the end the science of sciences is theology—
the knowing of God, revealed in Christ and in his creation.
Therefore, while in theory it is possible to devise an entirely
godless system of, say, secondary education, yet, in practice,
having in view the further stages of education, a non-religious,
even a non-Christian education is bound to prove unsatisfactory. And while defects may not appear in the earlier
stages, it seems necessary to infer that they will be latent.

This may seem to be contradicting what we have just said.
But it does not really do so, and we may elucidate the matter
by a comparison which recently I heard suggested to refute
the necessity for or even the possibility of a specifically
Christian education. The opponent urged that, after all,
education in its earlier stages, and especially in what we may
describe as "secular" subjects, is analogous to the manu-
facture of bricks, from which an edifice is to be constructed.
The bricks, it was pointed out, are substantially the same,
whether they are going to make a Gothic cathedral or a
Moslem mosque. It is all a question of how they are arranged
afterwards. The comparison is not a very good one, but accepting it for what it is worth, we are surely right in pointing out that the very size and shape and material of the
bricks are largely determined in accordance with their later
function. But St Thomas, on the principles we have been
discussing, would reject the whole force of the analogy.
Education is not the production of atoms of information in

isolation; it is simply the developing of an individual mind. And the perfection, the *telos* of that mind, must surely be allowed to condition the whole activity from the beginning. Now, in the order of nature, that *telos* will be the understanding of things in their ultimate causes, which we call philosophy. And to that extent, a humane non-religious education may be conceded to be a possibility. In fact, we may go further and urge that non-religious education may, up to a point, prove more satisfactory than a specifically religious training *which fails to see that religion, the supernatural, is only intelligible and acceptable when it keeps clearly in view its obligations to the natural.* But undoubtedly the perfect education can be devised only by those possessing the fullness of belief in Christian doctrine, which includes a due reverence for and appreciation of the value of the natural good—whether aesthetic, intellectual, or moral.

To invoke the authority of St Thomas in this matter, we may be allowed to develop what he says in answer to the objection that stimulating the intellect to know is only like stimulating the eye to see. He distinguishes within the mind different degrees of relation to intelligible objects. The mind sees certain things as self-evident; it may be said to have *habitual* knowledge of them, and they need only to be pointed out to it to be grasped clearly and certainly. St Thomas does not clearly specify the sphere of these objects. But I do not think we shall be doing violence to his thought by suggesting that he would include much mathematical and grammatical matter. In these departments the qualifications demanded of the ideal teacher will be not so much moral or religious as primarily psychological—his capacity to stimulate in his pupil that interest which will inspire him to "use his brains". The teacher is, then, not unlike one who stimulates another to "open his eyes" and to see. But for the rest, there is need of much inference: and here, clearly, error is more likely. Hence we shall need a teacher who, in addition to possessing the capacity for arousing interest, will also be himself conscientious in guiding the pupil to make the correct inferences:

not *imposing* his own beliefs, since that is not education: but standing by to prevent the pupil from drawing false conclusions, since the master has a responsibility to truth—that is ultimately to God. Hence we can understand how it is possible for a non-religious teacher, given conscientious devotion to truth, to be a better teacher in the earlier stages than a religious man who has not the same capacity for stimulating to activity the mind of his pupil. But, in the end, the whole process must be somehow controlled by those who are alive to the deepest demands of the whole man, and are not simply concerned to inculcate a certain mass of factual information.

At this stage there will undoubtedly be many who are wondering whether St Thomas has anything helpful to say to the person who accepts the need for an overruling religious control—whether immediate or remote—in the business of education, but is still in the dark as to the way in which education is possible at all. In this respect, the following passage from the third article of *De Magistro* may be worth studying: "Knowledge of unknown things is caused through principles intuitively known: in a way, then, man is the cause of another's knowing, not by giving the knowledge of principles but by educing into actuality that which is implicitly and in a certain way potentially contained in the principles, by means of sensible signs shown to the external senses. . . ." And, in the second article: "He who is the teacher must have explicitly and perfectly the knowledge which he causes in another. . . ." And lastly: "The words of the teacher have a closer relation to causing knowledge than have mere perceivable things outside the mind."

To appreciate the force of these passages adequately would, of course, involve a fairly exhaustive study of the Thomist psychology of the cognitive process—a long business. But perhaps we can briefly indicate some practical implications of his teaching which will suffice for our present purposes. In the first place when he speaks of the teacher's possessing "explicitly and perfectly" the knowledge which he causes in another, this cannot merely mean that the teacher has all the facts at his finger-tips. It is notorious that the most competent scholar is not infrequently the worst possible teacher. It may be ideally true that the "words of the teacher have a close relation to causing knowledge"; often they succeed in causing a fog! No. What it does seem to mean is that not only must the teacher possess "information", but he must possess it as *knowledge*; as something, in other words, which he sees in its relation to the human mind or, to use St Thomas's terminology, as an actualization of the mind's potentiality. Since, then, knowledge is nothing else than this, the true teacher will approach his task in that spirit of unselfish co-operation with the awakening mind of the pupil, which is perhaps always characteristic of the earnest teacher.

Admittedly there are very real difficulties. Where the unfortunate master or mistress has to "get through" a syllabus, teaching a class of pupils of very unequal mental calibre, the temptation to have recourse to the methods of the animal trainer sometimes becomes very strong indeed. Fortunately, there is a fairly widespread reaction from the school of thought which held that "knowledge maketh a bloody entrance". But the present state of things is unsatisfactory, precisely because modern educational theory is not sufficiently clear in its own mind as to the nature of human thinking. The insistence on self-development is all to the good. But it can be carried to excess—as in the type of school which, disregarding the fact of original sin, and apparently influenced by the Rousseauesque conception of man as born free and innocent, asserts that no sort of control or discipline is desirable. (One is reminded of the child in *Punch* being brought up on the most modern lines, and finally bursting out with: "Oh, Mummy, I do *wish* I could do something I don't want to do.")

No. Man's "educability"—that is, his capacity for realizing the fullness of his powers by self-activity—is, like all about him, subject to law and discipline. The very exuberance of his powers requires guidance and direction. Otherwise they will riot and run to seed. In an American edition of the *De*

Magistro there is this definition of man's educability: "The potentiality for the self-stabilization of human plasticity into an integrated character under the influence of an ideal." The human mind is "plastic"—it can be moulded: it is not predetermined. Because plastic, it is in some danger of instability: of a one-sided exaggeration of this or that aspect of the whole truth which man is made for. Hence the need for guidance—for teaching. But if teaching is directed towards the stabilization of the developing mind, it must never lose sight of the truth that, in the last analysis, it is a self-stabilization. Just as God himself respects the freedom he has conferred upon his creature, so must the teacher remember that he is, after all, but an extrinsic agent in the process of education.

But though the teacher is but an extrinsic agent, teaching is only possible because of the kinship existing between mind and mind. In any given mind the process of learning is the same: first comes the sense-experience, the apprehension of some visible, audible, tangible object, which I first of all dimly apprehend as a thing, as something not me, though in some mysterious way I make it mine, it enters into me: all I know at first is, perhaps, in the words of Professor James, "one big, blooming, buzzing confusion". Each feature of that confusion possesses significance. It is the teacher's task to direct the child's mind to this or that feature of it, features possessing a significance for the teacher, which he seeks somehow to "get across" to the child. How all that is to be done, how the child's mind is to be led on to draw for itself increasing "significances", how the growth of the child's mind is to be stimulated and encouraged without undue assertiveness on the part of the teacher, yet with no lack of the necessary firmness and guidance; what departments of knowledge are to be opened successively to the mind of the pupil—all these are questions of detail which it is not our present purpose to discuss. Much excellent work has been done in this department since the days of Pestalozzi. Pestalozzi himself, for instance, urged: "Let the child not only be acted upon, but let him be an *agent* in intellectual education." St Thomas would reinforce that by pointing out that, in fact, education is only possible where the child *is* an agent. And Spencer's remark: "It cannot be too strenuously insisted upon that in education the process of self-development should be encouraged to the fullest extent" adds nothing at all to the doctrine of *De Magistro*.

There is, however, one point of peculiar practical importance to be found in our analysis, and it may be worth while spending some little time on it. It is the question of "symbols" to which we referred at the beginning. For, while it has a practical bearing, it also reinforces the moral of this whole discussion. Symbols, by their very name, are related to something. To suggest that education consists merely in getting a lot of symbols—lists, schemes, diagrams etc.—"by heart" is rather like suggesting that to make a journey is merely to collect a whole lot of signposts. All objects are, in a real sense, "symbolic", inasmuch as they are particular expressions of a universal meaning. The mind, as we know, has the capacity to "abstract" that universal meaning from the particular; and the crux of the whole business of education is to devise a scheme of symbolic presentation which will ensure that the free activity of the pupil will be stimulated to know. "Hence", to quote St Thomas again, "one man is said to teach another because the teacher proposes to another by means of symbols the discursive process which he himself goes through by natural reason, and thus the natural reason of the pupil comes to a cognition of the unknown through the aid of what is proposed to him."

Perhaps the chief danger encountered in planning a syllabus or curriculum is that the teacher or planner may fail to appreciate the significance of those words "the discursive process which he himself goes through". Because the adult mind has come to hold its sum of knowledge in a synthetic unity, in which each element illustrates and integrates with the rest, we sometimes fail to realize that this result is the effect of a long process, and that we did not as a rule *learn* that way. And, what is more, as St Thomas reminds us, "all learning comes about through pre-existing knowledge". Which suggests that the secret of successful teaching is the finding of links between subjects: or, perhaps better, so arranging the syllabus or curriculum that, as we have already suggested, each subject leads on to the next, leaving in the child's mind a problem to be solved, a question to be answered.

CHAPTER X

THE IDEA OF
A UNIVERSITY

There is a passage at the end of one of T. S. Eliot's essays which may well serve as a sort of text to the following discussion. The essay is entitled "Tradition and the Individual Talent" and the passage sums up the thesis of that essay: "The emotion of art is impersonal; and the poet cannot reach this impersonality without surrendering himself wholly to the work to be done. And he is not likely to know what is to be done unless he lives in what is not merely the present, but the present moment of the past, unless he is conscious, not of what is dead but of what is already living."

It is true enough that, at least in our religious and philosophical thought, we Catholics have a remarkable, some would say an exaggerated respect for tradition. Our enemies accuse us of being conscious of what is dead rather than of what is already living. We know ourselves to be the heirs of a noble tradition. Such knowledge does undoubtedly carry with it very real dangers. The very title of this paper inevitably and rightly recalls the great utterances of John Henry Newman on the subject, addressed to a Dublin audience over a century ago. His words have become for many of us the very stuff of our thinking. The range and scope of his treatment is so comprehensive that we may be inclined to look back to them as containing all that we need to solve our present perplexities. But he himself would be the first to remind us that human thought and human knowledge do not stand still, that our appreciation even of the deposit of faith is a growing and developing thing, and that each generation, living in the present moment of the past must give itself utterly to the immediate work to be done.

What then is that work but the rethinking and restating of our heritage to a world that recks nothing of it? Yet we cannot do that unless, while we appreciate and love that heritage, we are at the same time sympathetic and understanding in our approach to the men of our own age. There are then two ways in which we may fail in our approach: one is by adopting the superior attitude of those who think they have all the answers, that the sad plight of the world is due entirely to the failure of men to listen to the great voices of the past, that, in a word, we have nothing to learn from our contemporaries; the other is by abandoning the past and seeking to adapt ourselves as closely as may be to the methods and outlook of those about us. In both cases, surely, we have failed to achieve that "impersonality" of which Eliot speaks, that sense of being dedicated to a high task, of immersing ourselves in the current of history, preserving alive all that is best in our traditions and vitalizing them still more by living contact with all that is best in our day. To quote Eliot again: "The difference between the present and the past is that the conscious present is an awareness of the past in a way and to an extent which the past's awareness of itself cannot show."

Let us begin then by refreshing our awareness of that past. And how better and how more fitly can we do it then by reminding ourselves of some of the great principles enunciated by Newman in his immortal Discourses? They are familiar to all of us, so familiar indeed that there may be some danger of their becoming, as Coleridge puts it, "bedridden in the dormitory of the soul". It is, one may guess, the Discourse "Knowledge Its Own End", which Newman delivered with the greatest satisfaction and to which we ourselves should turn with the greatest enthusiasm. For while his profoundly religious soul appreciated the fitness of delivering the first discourse on "Theology a Branch of Knowledge", and while we all naturally accept the appropriateness of its position, and are indeed certain that there can be no complete system of thought which does not fit into a general framework of religious truth, that very conviction may, if we are not careful, lessen in our eyes the value of knowledge for its own sake. We are all familiar with the type of person who, with an awful glibness, dismisses as ephemeral the pursuit of "secular" knowledge, suggesting indeed that such knowledge is a threat to one's eternal salvation. St Thomas Aquinas, we are told, after writing his *Summa* and the other works displaying his knowledge and his passionate interest in every aspect of the truth, confessed that all that he had written seemed to him but chaff. But the fact remains that he *had* written the *Summa*. May it not be that such passionate pursuit of the truth for its own sake is a pre-condition of the later vision?

No one will be tempted to call in question the unworldliness of Cardinal Newman, who sacrificed so much of worldly prospects in pursuit of the highest ideals. Yet none has pleaded more eloquently than he for the autonomy of learning:

> Surely it is very intelligible to say, and that is what I say here, that Liberal Education, viewed in itself, is simply the cultivation of the intellect, as such, and its object is nothing more or less than intellectual eminence. Everything has its own perfection, be it higher or lower in the scale of things; and the perfection of one is not the perfection of another. . . . The artist puts before him beauty of feature and form; the poet, beauty of mind; the preacher, the beauty of grace; the intellect, too, I repeat, has its beauty and it has those who aim at it. To open the mind, to correct it, to refine it, to enable it to know, and to digest, master, rule and use its knowledge, to give it power over its own faculties, application, flexibility, method, critical exactness, sagacity, resource, address, eloquent expression, is an object as intelligible . . . as the cultivation of virtue, while, at the same time, it is absolutely distinct from it. This is indeed but a temporal object, and a transitory possession; but so are other things in themselves which we make much of and pursue. . . . We attain to heaven by using

this world well, though it is to pass away; we perfect our nature, not by undoing it, but by adding to it what is more than nature, and directing it towards aims higher than its own.

It is by that principle we must be guided if we are to foster aright or to renew in our minds the Idea of a University. Newman, as we know, for all his serene grasp of fundamentals, did not delude himself into thinking that all was well with university studies in his own day. On the contrary, he was fully alive to the dangers implicit in the very attempt to teach "universal knowledge" which he declared to be the function of the university. The very opportunities for advanced education brought with them their own error:

> The error of distracting and enfeebling the mind by an unmeaning profusion of subjects; of implying that a smattering in a dozen branches of study is not shallowness, which it really is, but enlargement, which it is not; of considering an acquaintance with the learned names of things and persons and the possession of clever duodecimos, and attendance on eloquent lectures, and membership with scientific institutions, and the sight of the experiments of a platform and the specimens of a museum, that all this was not dissipation of mind but progress. . . .

If that was true a hundred years ago, how much greater is the danger to-day. When Newman was a Fellow of Oriel, I suppose the number of faculties in the university would amount to scarcely half a dozen. To-day Oxford has some twenty faculties, with an enormous list of Professors, Lecturers and Readers. Societies by the score, technical journals by the hundred, an increasing mass of detailed information to be absorbed by the candidate for a First Class—all these are features of university life which would terrify us had we not become conditioned to the acceptance of them as the normal thing. Is this process to be allowed to go on unchecked, or can we hope to slow down the tempo of academic life, to restore something of that leisureliness of mind which would seem to be essential to that true perfection which Newman hymns so eloquently?

Again let Newman speak:

> The perfection of the intellect which is the result of education
> and its *beau ideal,* to be imparted to individuals in their re-
> spective measures, is the clear, calm, accurate vision and com-
> prehension of all things, as far as the finite mind can embrace
> them, each in its own place, and with its own characteristics
> upon it. It is almost prophetic from its knowledge of history;
> it is almost heart-searching from its knowledge of human
> nature; it has almost supernatural charity from its freedom
> from littleness and prejudices; it has almost the repose of faith
> because nothing can startle it; it has almost the beauty and
> harmony of heavenly contemplation, so intimate is it with the
> eternal order of things and the music of the spheres.

In an age when so much intellectual effort, material equipment and human energy is devoted to the development of
scientific research which brings so many perils in its train,
when scholarship so often becomes the tool of propaganda,
when philosophy is degraded by an even more arid form of
Nominalism than the fourteenth century knew, or is per-
verted by a false and pessimistic psychology, when even
theology herself is all too often corrupted by sophistry and
scepticism, we may well be tempted to despair of our task
and take refuge in an attitude of anti-intellectualism. We recall, perhaps, that in the early centuries of her history the
Church experienced a similar temptation to turn her back
on the learning and culture all about her, and in the deserts
of Egypt and Syria, to work out her salvation in solitude and
silence. But, fortunately for herself and for Europe, there
were great men and great minds who knew that the schools
of Athens and Alexandria, of Rome and Milan, had their
contribution to make to the understanding and elucidation
of the truth revealed in Christ, and where Clement and Cyril,
Athanasius, Ambrose and Augustine have led the way, we
must encourage ourselves to follow. In a later century too
it was felt by a large number of eminent men that theology
had no part in dialectic, that Christian truth could learn
nothing from pagan thought. It is the glory of Aquinas that
he refused to accept such a diminishing of truth. Through

him and through the medieval universities was established
once for all the principle that there must be no fear of knowledge in any form. You may feel that it is time to call a halt,
that the very ideal of a pursuit of universal knowledge has
resulted in a situation in which the ideal defeats itself, that
in trying to learn everything we succeed in learning nothing
well or, by a natural reaction, we come to specialize so nar-
rowly that the mind becomes no less impoverished. But the
remedy for such a situation is not to throw over the ideal but
to see how best it can be maintained. It is not the ideal that
is at fault but we who, somehow, have become unfitted to
pursue it. It is we who need to be changed.

This does not mean that there is need of any radical reformation of our attitude to knowledge. On the contrary, it is
one of the most heartening features of the situation that the
human mind remains, in essence, indestructible, indefatigable
in its quest for truth, unyielding in its conviction that the
great jewel of truth is beyond price. Even those who seek to
corrupt and enslave the minds of others can only succeed in
some small measure by playing on this abiding fact. Propaganda, however false it may be, can only condition men's
minds to its acceptance, in so far as it is based on some
semblance of objectivity. That is why all false systems contain within themselves the seeds of decay. For it is in the
nature of things that men hate and reject deception or even
ignorance about ultimate reality, as Plato reminds us. In a
society where the organs of public instruction are rigidly
controlled by unscrupulous politicians, it is possible for a time
to keep men in a state of confusion and uncertainty about
contemporary events. It is even possible to indoctrinate them
with false principles of action, to present a one-sided and
distorted view of life and its purpose. But the deeper you go,
the more difficult does it become to carry conviction. Sooner
or later the revulsion must come.

So too in the academic sphere. However superficial and
trivial may seem to be so much of what today passes for
philosophy, however incomplete and partial may be the pic-

ture of human life drawn by the historian or the psychologist, however perilous be the materialistic outlook of the physical scientist, these aspects of truth (for they are such) do have their part to play in the grand design. Whether or not we can go all the way with Sir Walter Moberley's plea for completely unfettered speculation in a university whose prime duty is the education of those whose inexperience unfits them to select and sift true from false, worthless from worthwhile, we cannot doubt the nobility which inspires such an appeal. For we must remember that our appreciation of truth, even of the truth revealed in Christ, is a growing and expanding thing. At no stage can we human beings claim to be in a position to erect barriers, to say, here we have reached the very confines of knowledge, beyond this point no advance is possible. Where some new proposal involves a denial of what we know to be true, we may and indeed must protest. We must remind the sceptic that we have grounds for our faith not less valid than his own presuppositions, and we are entitled to appeal to his own principles of toleration and unprejudiced desire for truth which may suggest to him, if he is sincere, that our own contribution may be not less important than his own. But we on our side must have the courage of our convictions. We do well to recall the words spoken by Newman well nigh a hundred years ago:

> I say, then, he who believes Revelation with that absolute faith which is the prerogative of a Catholic, is not the nervous creature who startles at every sudden sound, and is flustered by every strange or novel appearance which meets his eyes. He has no sort of apprehension, he laughs at the idea, that anything can be discovered by any other scientific method, which can contradict any one of the dogmas of his religion . . . this, gentlemen, is why I say that to erect a University is at once so arduous and beneficial an undertaking, viz., because it is pledged to admit, without fear, without prejudice, without compromise, all comers, if they come in the name of Truth; to adjust views, and experiences, and habits of mind the most independent and dissimilar; and to give full play to thought and erudition in their most original forms, and their most intense expressions, and in their most ample circuit. Thus

to draw many things into one, is its special function; and it learns to do it, not by rules reducible to writing, but by sagacity, wisdom, and forbearance, acting upon a profound insight into the subject matter of knowledge and by a vigilant repression of aggression or bigotry in any quarter.

That is nobly uttered. There are few of us who do not need to take it to heart. The very utterance of such a principle evokes from us all a response which, again, may hearten us to our task. I mean by this that, despite the apparent gulf that separates our world from his, despite the many features of contemporary life—the myriad applications of scientific discovery which have so transformed the habits of modern man that we are sometimes tempted to think of him as a different sort of being—we recognize a deep kinship with the mind of a thinker whose vocabulary did not include a single one of many words which are on the lips of every schoolboy —motor-car, petrol, wireless, aeroplane, switch, bus, television set, atomic energy, jet propulsion, sound-track, lift, or even electric toaster. The externals of life may seem to affect us profoundly. For all that, the human mind is the same sort of thing that it has ever been. These things are a product of its ingenuity. They are its creatures; it remains unaffected by them in its essential nature.

And that is why it is relevant to go far back beyond Newman himself, beyond even the foundation of the university as we know it, to the teaching of Plato. His teaching on education is still important and it can help us in our present undertaking. Let us recall the salient features of the discussion of this subject in the *Republic*. In the first place, we must bear in mind the distinction he makes between the education of the ordinary citizen and that of the special class of "rulers". The modern principle of equality of opportunity does not invalidate the obvious fact that only a relatively small proportion of mankind is really equipped for higher education. We should all probably agree that anyone who is suited by natural endowment should be given such opportunity and we must be grateful for recent advances in this matter. At the same time, we must always bear in mind the undoubted fact that the general level of education in a community will, in the end, depend upon the attainment of a higher level by a minority. We may therefore take it that Plato's discussion of the education of the "rulers" has reference to our own problem of university education. Now the remarkable feature of Plato's treatment is that he clearly thought that higher education, as we understand it, should not begin until the student had reached the age of twenty, and that it should continue for the next ten years, at which stage a further selection should be made. Philosophy proper —the crown of education—should not begin until the student has reached the age of thirty, and should then continue for five years. Admittedly, as Socrates implies more than once, he is discussing the problem in a sort of theoretical world, where time does not seem to matter very much, and looked at in the cold light of practicality such suggestions carry with them an air of the ludicrous. Yet Plato clearly has his feet very much on the ground, and his suggestions are related to the actual qualities of human nature. In his view, as in Aristotle's, young men are not fit persons for philosophical activity. For youngsters, as he says—"when they first get the taste of argument into their mouths, use it for fun, for ever objecting, refuting others in imitation of those who refute them; they are like little puppies, taking pleasure in pulling and tearing at others by way of arguing". This breeds irresponsibility and ultimately scepticism.

No one who has had experience of undergraduate societies will question the truth of this observation. Does it then follow that we must abolish the Greats School and the Moral Philosophy Tripos, and leave the business of philosophy to dons? Hardly that, though a more serious attention to Plato's ideas might warn many philosophy tutors of the great responsibility they bear in this matter. They must surely bear in mind more clearly than they seem to do that intellectual precocity often goes hand in hand with moral immaturity, and that skill in dialectic is quite compatible with lack of judgement.

If Plato's own remedy is too drastic, at least let us pay him the compliment of heeding his warnings and seeking to profit by his wisdom. The passage in the sixth book of the *Republic* in which he analyses the steps by which the philosophical nature corrupts is as pertinent today as it was in fifth century Athens. The capacity to stand out against the pressure of public opinion and to resist the influence of the prevailing mental climate is the rarest endowment.

And yet, as Plato himself saw, somehow, under the providence of God, the good does survive and somehow men do achieve a solid sound education. How precisely Plato conceived that providence to work we cannot say. But at least the modern European, if he is intelligent enough, can hardly deny the role which the Church has played in the defence of human sanity. It was she who protected the heritage of Greece and Rome against the Hun and the Turk; it was she who assimilated the literary and artistic achievement of that ancient world, who defended the Aristotelian system from Moslem misrepresentation; she it was who educated the Frank and the Saxon, who established schools and universities in the midst of barbarism; for centuries she was the sole cultural and educational force in Europe, and the modern unbeliever owes immeasurably more to her achievement than he is prepared to confess. And today, when great searchings of heart are taking place in the West, we can hardly doubt that she will still be called upon to play her traditional part.

That is why we Catholics need to think and rethink our position in this matter. Some of us may be tempted to ask whether the time is not ripe for the establishment of a Catholic university. The ancient English universities have to a large extent forgotten their origins, and the modern foundations have never known the traditions upon which our civilization has been based. Ought we not then to say: Let us withdraw from an alien and unsympathetic world and build for ourselves a new home of learning, where we may cultivate in security and peace our familiar arts and teach to our own children the ancient wisdom of the Church? How many

Catholics are tempted by such a vision it is difficult to say: but it should not be too readily accepted.

In the first place, even were the necessary means at hand for the foundation of such an institution on a worthy scale, it seems impossible that we should be able to find teachers of adequate ability in sufficient numbers to make the education there anything but second-rate. But even if these difficulties could be surmounted, there remain two most important considerations which seem to render such a scheme undesirable. In the first place it would be a refusal of what is, after all, a primary duty of the Christian—to act as leaven in the world. We are supremely privileged in being heirs to a great tradition, in possessing in an outstanding way that truth which, as we have seen, is the object of man's intellectual searchings. Are we then to hug this treasure to our self-satisfied bosoms and refuse to share with others the wealth that we possess? Or are we not rather fired with the ambition to co-operate to the utmost in this common purpose? Secondly, it seems certain that we ourselves should be the losers if we accepted such a proposal.

If there is one lesson that history should have taught us, it is that the truth develops best when there is clash of mind upon mind, when different points of view, passionately held and fiercely defended, front each other in ardent debate. And while it is true that there is wide room for divergence of opinion within the realm of purely Catholic thought, it is equally true that the skeleton of dogma tends to ossify and lose its flexibility where it is not subjected to the pressure of attack and questioning, calling out the response of elucidation and defence. Where a tradition is taken for granted and is maintained without effort, that tradition loses something of vitality and freshness. If the price of liberty is eternal vigilance, an analogous reflection will suggest that we must be ever on the watch lest, with no threat to be countered, we lose that true freedom of thought which is ours, only when we are under the necessity of fighting in its defence. Believing as we do that it is the possession of the truth that makes us free, we should be glad to feel called to fight that fight. It has to be admitted that this argument traverses a policy which, in other countries, has established universities for Catholics, taught by Catholics; but it is not the result of nationalistic or local patriotism which prompts us to hold that if such institutions are to flourish they need to maintain vital and intimate contact with universities of a wider character.

Obviously, the presence of Catholic undergraduates at non-Catholic universities raiscs spccial problems, and undoubtedly we need to give time to a consideration of those problems. Clearly, too, an indiscriminate admission of Catholics to certain universities would not be desirable, any more than it is desirable to impose upon weak characters tests which they are incapable of enduring. But it would be a sad day for the Church when it ceased to be lawful for its members to attend, under proper safeguards, universities of a genuinely liberal character. Needless to say, these views are no more than the expression of a personal point of view, which may be deemed too bold, and which many readers will doubtless wish to question. And it must be confessed that we here seem to have deserted our master, John Henry Newman, whose Introductory Discourse was very largely a defence of the plan of founding precisely such a Catholic university. But we may question whether, had he but lived a few years longer, he would not have rejoiced more than any other at the decision of the hierarchy which, in 1895, permitted Catholics to attend the universities of Great Britain, and whether he would not have seen in that step the beginning of the realization of the dreams he had outlined in his Irish Discourses.

However that may be, we may well pass on to consider how we may best hope to realize the ideals he there expounded. The first duty we have is to bring home to ourselves the paramount importance of aiming at that intellectual eminence for which he pleaded with so much fervour. We who base our whole hope here and hereafter on the belief that the eternal

Wisdom of God became incarnate for our sakes and walked this earth in human guise must see to it that we cherish within ourselves that creaturely participation in the uncreated being of God which is our high privilege. Any purely utilitarian or pragmatic approach to truth is doubly unworthy of a Christian man because it is unworthy of any human being. We should be shamed by the self-forgetting devotion of the scholar to his learning, of the scientist to his research, of the metaphysician to his unending quest. Just as, in another sphere, the neglect by Christians of the burning problems of social justice has been a source of untold harm, so has our failure in the past to seek after truth constituted a betrayal which has resulted in the sorry state of things we see at present. The pursuit of knowledge has become secularized because our possession of revealed truth tempted us to laziness of mind. Admittedly, there are many extenuating circumstances. We can point to the many handicaps under which the Catholic body in Britain has laboured for the last three centuries and more. Admitting all that, we must still maintain that we could and should have done so much more than we have achieved. It is surely significant that the men and women of intellectual eminence in the Church in this country are, to an overwhelming extent, converts—those reared in another tradition and another atmosphere.

If then those of us who are privileged to belong to a university faculty or who are otherwise concerned with the business of educating the young can develop within ourselves some of that passion for the things of the mind we can hope to promote that intellectual Second Spring which is so long overdue. More than that, we shall take our place naturally and easily in the world of letters, no longer somewhat self-conscious newcomers but finding ourselves in the company of colleagues and collaborators. With admiration for their integrity and sympathy with their ideals, we shall enter into the great fellowship of those who are devoted to the cause of learning, which is the cause of truth. Where we encounter suspicion and hostility, due, at least to some extent, to our own shortcomings in the past, our unaffected enthusiasm and obvious singlemindedness will go far to dispel the prejudice against our alleged obscurantism and the doubts about our sincerity.

What, finally, *is* a university? Newman, you will recall, defined it as a place for teaching universal knowledge. But that clearly is a highly idealized definition. There never was such a place. From the earliest times there was always a tendency to specialize, to teach law at Bologna, medicine at Montpellier, theology at Paris, and so on. It is a tendency which has become accentuated as the scope of human knowledge has become enlarged. Perhaps a university cannot be "defined": perhaps it is better to dwell on the common aspects of teaching and of thought which should unite those, who are, wherever they may find themselves, to constitute a true fellowship. That fellowship can be fostered and maintained only where there is an acceptance of a common body of principles. In its explicit form such an acceptance involves the formal recognition of a theological framework, the belief in theology as queen of the sciences. But we are surely right in holding that wherever men are gathered together in sincerity to discover and hand on the truth, there is a true university. Its members will be distinguished by a spirit of self-sacrifice to a common ideal, without prejudice and without fear, sincere, patient, possessing on the natural plane the qualities which, supernaturalized, constitute what we call Christian charity. For we should never forget that the human mind is, in Tertullian's phrase, *naturaliter Christiana*. In such men we find our natural allies. The world's need is desperate; its wounds can in the end be healed by no one but Christ. But he works through us. Let us, whose vocation is an intellectual one, find in the discipline of the mind the asceticism which will fit us to play our part in the total work of his Body.

CHAPTER XI

PREPARING FOR
THE UNIVERSITY[1]

In the following pages I have tried to answer the question: How best can we prepare young people for life in a modern university?

One obvious difficulty in making recommendations to those actually in charge of day-to-day education is that they may seem almost unrelated to the hard facts of school life. Let me say at once, therefore, that I am fully alive to the fact that we are living in an imperfect world, in which the realization of any ideal is bound to be frustrated by certain harsh realities. I might sketch out an elaborate curriculum which would be directed towards the production of the model undergraduate. But it is no use turning out model undergraduates unless you can get them accepted by a university or a university college. And that means getting the candidate through an intricate series of examinations. I shall try, therefore, to aim at making suggestions which will not involve additions to an over-crowded syllabus and a time-table already as complicated as the maze at Hampton Court.

Secondly, I have a simple but profound faith in the actuality of original sin. Training animals is child's play compared to the task of educating the young in the way they ought to go. We can attend lectures on human psychology, on the latest educational methods, on the place which the liturgy ought to occupy in our schools, on German or French or Dutch

[1] Based on an address to nuns engaged in teaching.

catechetics, on the importance of apologetics, on the futility of apologetics, but all this has got to be applied to human beings. And how unpredictable human beings are! We must all have had sufficient experience of the way in which the carefully prepared lesson misfires completely, while the impromptu illustration, the casual aside, is the one thing which is remembered and quoted back at us, years after, by pupils whom we have almost forgotten. How difficult it is to persuade the young to share our views as to what is interesting or important! We can perhaps take comfort from the thought that the greatest of all teachers had one shocking failure out of a class of twelve, even after three years of constant indoctrination; while some of the others were somewhat unsatisfactory specimens.

And even when, with the help of God and the expenditure of limitless quantities of sweat and tears and even blood, we have cultivated our garden so well that we can count on half-a-dozen perfect specimens, we are still at the mercy of that malign perversity which besets the life of man. Either the College examiners are curiously blind to the merits of our children, or they admit them but want them to read some subject for which we think they are not fitted. Or the undergraduate contracts some malady or is involved in a car smash or becomes the victim of some disaster completely outside her control.

I am, you see, trying to be realistic, to emphasize the simple truth that in life there are no short cuts. It would be folly to suppose that we are likely overnight to raise the general standard of university performance by Catholic undergraduates to any marked extent. Life is not like that. On the other hand, I am quite certain that there is a real value in this sort of discussion. For human civilization is, like the coral island, a slow, almost imperceptible growth—the achievement of a countless number of individuals working together, each making a tiny contribution. Despite difficulties and setbacks of every kind the work goes forward.

"The froth being out of the bottle" in George Meredith's

phrase, let us turn to our task. Making due allowance for all that I have said hitherto, it will still be profitable to think for a time in terms of the ideal product. What, then, is the sort of undergraduate we ought to be trying to turn out? Obviously, one possessed of a mind that has been trained to analyse critically, to assess evidence judicially, to think constructively. One, moreover, who, for all his intellectual ability, knows perfectly well that life is more than scholarship; who lives in no ivory tower, but is willing to go down into the market-place, to share in the interests of others, to learn from companions as well as from books, to relate his specialized learning to the general needs of mankind; one who is humble in the face of his task, and yet confident in his ability to succeed; who is mature and wise, and yet natural and unsophisticated; who is honest and openminded, yet able to defend and hold fast to the certainties he has acquired; fastidious without pretentiousness, confident without affectation, serene without insensitivity.

We turn from the contemplation of this paragon to the thought of the actual products as we know them—all too often, either narrow specialists who have no influence on their fellow-students because they have no realization of the interests of others, or else superficial minds who, having scraped into the university by dint of cramming, never seem to grow in intellectual stature, and dissipate their talents in a round of futile activities. Unable to keep the true balance between the things of the mind and the wider interest of the human scene, they rarely develop into harmoniously integrated beings. It they succeed in getting a good degree it is too often at the expense of achievements in other fields; more commonly they fail to do justice to themselves academically because they have been swept off their feet by the glamour of the wider aspects of university life.

You are perhaps thinking that I am straying from my text. My subject is the spiritual formation of these young people, and here I am discussing academic standards and the like. Yet I am sure that what I have been saying is highly germane.

In so far as we do fail, in so far, that is, as the failures of our children are to be laid at our doors, it may well be because we have thought too much in compartments. We have sought, perhaps, to train our children in secular knowledge—languages, history, science, geography—and to add a top dressing of "spiritual formation" through sodalities, retreats and the like. (Let me hasten to add that I am not suggesting that any of these activities are not desirable; I am merely insisting that they fail in their full effect because they are kept in a separate compartment.)

Broadly speaking I believe it is true to say that our children are influenced far more by what we ourselves *are* than by anything that we *say*. I am not forgetting the immense importance of the home background on the development of a pupil's personality; but I am convinced that a really inspiring teacher can have a crucial impact on the growth of his spiritual outlook, no less than on his intellectual formation. Indeed, my whole point is that, in the end, the two—intellectual formation and spiritual growth, are inextricably involved.

Take for example the individual's attitude to the faith. What is it, in the end, that makes one person balanced and serene in her adherence, another liable to recurrent crises, a third sceptical and, at times, hostile? There is no single explanation. But I am sure that the greatest contribution we can make in this matter is to ensure that the child's growth in maturity in learning and experience is not allowed to outstrip her understanding of the content of the faith. "Simple" faith is so often a retarded faith. A human being whose mental age is seventeen or eighteen must have an approach to the faith of an equal maturity. Let us ask ourselves whether perhaps we do not expect our children to be negative and unquestioning in this most vital of all matters at a time when we are encouraging them to be critical and inquisitive in other fields.

I have been haunted for years by the case of a young woman who came to see me at Oxford to discuss her problems. She told me that she had been educated at a convent

(I never asked her which one it was) and that in her last year at school she had had intellectual difficulties. When she told the nuns this, they pooh-poohed them and told her not to be silly. As she insisted they asked a priest to see her. He took the same attitude, with the result that she had not practised her religion for several years. A Catholic friend at Oxford persuaded her to come and see me, and fortunately she was able to see light and returned to Catholic practice.

Now I have no doubt that she was a tiresome child and that she may have been showing off or something like that. But I still think that she should not have been handled the way she was handled, and that a serious attempt should have been made to answer her questions. Much of the trouble in this sort of situation springs from the fact that the child senses in us a reluctance to discuss problems because we are unsure of ourselves, or because we are afraid to allow the child to ask questions about the faith. We have been told that "temptations against faith are to be treated like temptations against purity"—that is, by running away from them. I do not know what the theological justification for this principle is supposed to be; I am quite certain that it is psychologically unsound. I hold that a child has not merely a right, but a duty to ask questions, because it is only by asking questions that we show our aliveness to the importance of the subject-matter.

Let us then be ready to encourage questions; but let us be no less ready to try to answer them. (Fortunately there is a great advance being made in the theological education of nuns, and in the coming years we shall be better and better equipped to deal with these situations.) Yet the really important thing is not that we shall have a slick answer ready; what does matter is that we shall display genuine honesty and the right sort of openmindedness in our discussion of any question that may be raised. A child invariably knows when he is being fobbed off with an answer that has not been thought out, but which we hope will satisfy the questioner. Much better to admit frankly that we don't know the answer than to try to hedge. Otherwise he begins to think that it is not possible to defend the faith rationally, for all the assertions we make to the contrary. He develops a feeling of insecurity and when he is faced with the really searching questions of non-Catholic or agnostic fellow-undergraduates he will not have that sense of absolute conviction which he will need if he is to defend his faith to his own and to their satisfaction.

This is an example of what I mean when I say that children are influenced far more by what we are than by what we say. If they see us serene and secure in our faith, able to face questions and difficulties honestly and frankly, convinced that there *is* an answer whether we happen to know it or not, refusing to say anything which is an insult to the intelligence of a pupil whom we expect to compete with the products of the best schools in the country, then we shall have gone a long way towards developing in them maturity of belief comparable to the maturity of judgement which teachers look for in our candidates. You see, the pupil who is expected to discuss with insight the causes of the Reformation or the character of Iago is obviously a person who needs to be treated in an adult way in the all-important sphere of religion.

When we talk of "spiritual formation" we often make the mistake of thinking that all that is necessary is to encourage in those for whom we are responsible a habit of prayer and the sacraments. We apparently suppose that when we have got them into such habits, all is well. We are surprised and shocked when our "best pupils" suddenly collapse, become slack or even lapse altogether. We are forgetting that grace does not normally supply for the deficiencies of nature. What it does is to give to our natural qualities or activities an added virtue. But we need to look to the foundations of character, the natural basis of supernatural energizing.

The first thing we have to do is to try to develop in our charges a profound sense of responsibility. It is often alleged against the products of our Catholic schools—both boys and girls—that when they come up to a university they are liable to be wilder, more irresponsible, sillier than their opposite numbers from other establishments. I don't know what justification there is for this allegation, but I am quite certain that anyone who comes up to a university needs to be prepared for the wider freedom and the immensely richer variety of attractions that it offers. How is this to be done? The actual exercise of responsibility will vary according to the nature of the school. A day school provides more opportunities than does a boarding school, where the pupils are almost invariably aware of the presence in the background—and sometimes not even in the background—of the reproving eye of authority. We have to take real risks, give genuine freedom, provide something of the real challenge that life is so soon to offer.

It is not enough to give them authority, as prefects or monitors, over the younger children. This is often no more than an opportunity for giving vent to that sense of power which we all enjoy. It must be all a part of a progressive training in initiative and self-reliance. They must be given the sort of freedom which, used aright, will bring its own reward, but which, if abused, brings its own sanctions. For this is a law of life; and the sooner they learn it, in all its harsh reality, the better. The less we can make them feel that they are disappointing *us,* the less we give way to the temptation to interfere, the less we nag or threaten or punish the better. They must be made to feel that our trust in them is absolute, that we are not *pretending* to give them freedom. We must have the courage and generosity analogous to the divine trust which has left us with our free wills to make or mar our own lives.

Take for example the question of study. Within the framework of a planned syllabus to be covered in a certain period of time, there should always be found room for a piece of work—an essay of some length, a programme of reading, an individual job—which is the pupil's personal and sole responsibility. He may be encouraged to discuss it, to get advice, to report progress; he must be made to feel that this is his own effort. It is not even that he is told or made to feel that he is being "trusted" to make proper use of his time. The idea and the habit of making the best use of his opportunities must grow up, unselfconsciously. Let us not moralize about it to him, or encourage him in any kind of priggish sense of moral superiority. Let the sense of achievement be his reward, even while a word of encouragement or congratulation may, in due season, be added.

Similarly with the more practical charges we give them. How maddening it is to see work done less well or more slowly or more ineptly than we could do it ourselves! How tempting it is to interfere, to take over, to show our superior efficiency or experience! How firm we need to be with *ourselves,* more than with them! *Let* them make mistakes; it is often the only way to learn. *Let* them waste *our* time as well as their own; it will be a school of virtue for us even while it is being a school of experience for them.

Here again, of course, the influence of the home is a paramount factor. But we must be prepared to supply for the deficiencies of the home training or to ensure that our contribution does not lag behind it. Nor can I presume to descend to details, to indicate ways in which all this can be done. All I am doing is to plead for a certain attitude of mind. Granted that, the details will work themselves out. Remember, then, that when a young man (or woman) begins his university career, he will to a large extent have to manage his own life. This is an art which cannot be acquired overnight. Success depends on a long, progressive course of emancipation. Christ prayed: "I am not asking that thou shouldst take them out of the world, but that thou shouldst keep them clear of what is evil." The task of educators is to prepare their charges for the world in which they are to live. For that, you have been given a rule and a spirit. That rule and that spirit are to be preserved and yet interpreted as flexibly as possible, to be sure that they do not defeat their very purpose. However progressively-minded we may be, we are all, inevitably, under the influence of the system of education and the climate of opinion in which we ourselves were trained. It is well that this is so. Mankind needs always the anchor of tradition to prevent its being driven headlong in the direction of the prevailing wind.

Nevertheless, we must be equally ready to understand the changing situations as they arise, and to meet them with courage and broadmindedness. Much there is in university life which we may be right in condemning; the secularism, the scepticism, the readiness to challenge the basic Christian assumptions, the all too frequent denial of moral absolutes. Yet, when all is said and done, these are the defects of certain important virtues. Tolerance, openmindedness, honesty and the ability to appreciate another's point of view—all these are valuable and important. Nor do I believe that to a balanced and intelligent undergraduate the dangers of university life are anything like as grave as is sometimes assumed. These dangers may be thought of as either intellectual or moral. It is not, in my opinion, possible to delimit them as precisely as all that. To the person who is emotionally stable and morally balanced, such intellectual problems as may arise can be solved with no great difficulty, while he who appreciates the basic principles in which the Church's moral teaching is grounded and who has been trained in loyalty and self-discipline, the grosser forms of immorality he encounters are more likely to repel than to attract.

I have already spoken of the intellectual training of the future undergraduate, but this would seem to be the place for a discussion of moral training. Some of this ground too has been covered in what I said before about developing a sense of responsibility. Something remains to be said about the narrower but important field of sexual morality. Not that the age-long problems associated with this subject are specifically different at a university than they are elsewhere, except possibly that the pseudo-intellectual attack on Christian teaching may be more to the fore. This means that our training in this matter must be intelligent and rational. Adolescents must be made to see the *point* of purity, the wisdom of modesty, the positive force of high standards of conduct.

For, as I see it, the merely negative approach, the catalogue of forbidden acts, the tariff of sins beloved of the moral theologian is not only unhelpful but may be positively dangerous. If an adolescent is told, for example, that in certain cases kissing is mortally sinful, she may decide that, having crossed that particular Rubicon, there is no reason why she should not go much further. The impression I have formed over the years is that—for whatever reason—most teenagers think of purity in terms of what they may do without committing sin.

Is it not possible to develop a more constructive approach to what is, admittedly, a difficult problem? Should we not stress throughout our instructions the dignity of sex, the fact that through its use men and women find fulfilment, that in God's creative scheme it ranks as high as aesthetic satisfaction, that it is as precious as food and drink, which are not debased in themselves just because there happen to be gluttons and drunkards? We must not hesitate to let them see that we recognize the attraction they feel for the other sex— an attraction which will not diminish at the university—as a stage in the process of God's unfolding plan for them. Let us appeal first to the natural safeguards such as their own fastidiousness (which we are trying to develop in other compartments too), their sense of their own dignity and a proper pride in their own personal worth. It is never too early for them to begin to realize that human love is a priceless treasure, to be protected from all cheapening and degradation by any conduct which is unworthy of themselves, and of the love that is God's gift. Just as we train them to play their part in promoting the success of their school, just as we are preparing them to take their full part in the life of the country to which they belong, so they should be encouraged to realize that an important part of that contribution is their progressive growth and development as human beings, as men and women.

An aggravation of what has always been a difficult problem is due to the fact that, at school and especially in a convent, teenagers may develop a sort of divided mind on the subject of sex. In this uninhibited age, wherever they go, they are constantly coming up against more or less crude stimulations of sexual curiosity—in newspapers and periodicals, in various forms of entertainment, in conversations overheard, or even joined in, by them. At school the subject is very largely and quite rightly taboo. They may come to think us stuffy or straitlaced or too innocent for this world. What we have to do, without lowering our own standards, is to make them aware that we understand the world in which they live, that our reticence springs from an appreciation of the beauty of something that can so easily be coarsened, and not from fear or prudishness.

But probably the most important factor in the promotion of a healthy attitude to sex is the development of emotional stability. Where a child enjoys the stability of a happy home and is respected and genuinely appreciated at school, there is every chance that he will grow up without that perhaps half-conscious craving for sympathy and admiration which is so often the beginning of a dangerous friendship. There is clearly no short cut, no ready-made formula to deal with this aspect of a complex problem. But we have gone some way towards a solution if we understand the underlying psychological situation.

And so we come to the specifically spiritual element in our work of formation. Here we are to a great extent at the mercy of the different priests who give annual retreats, days of recollection, conferences and the like. We can't do much about that, except to be as discreet as we can in selecting those whom we invite. We can, however, collaborate with them by ourselves understanding and helping our children to understand the rôle of the supernatural in their lives. They must be encouraged to see the whole Christian dispensation as a power coming in to complete and extend the whole scope of natural values. They must, once again, be shown that being a good Christian does not mean primarily just keeping out of sin, or even performing a set of activities in the way of church-going, saying prayers and the like. They must learn that the whole significance and value of these lies in the fact that they are the external expression of an interior attitude.

Take for instance the much canvassed question of compulsory daily Mass in our boarding schools or monthly confessions in our day schools. Much can be said on either side, but I have myself no sort of doubt that we have failed in our duty if we can get our children to Mass or confession only under compulsion. I know how difficult it is when you are dealing with a herd not to fall back on herd-methods. But unless we can get our children to recognize that, if they cannot be said to want to go freely they ought at least to want to want it, I cannot see the point of their being there at all. I am aware of course, that the Church's law of Sunday observance is a form of compulsion, and that her children fulfil their obligation, as we say, by being there at all, from whatever motive. But not even the most rabid Catholic statistician really believes that the spiritual state of a parish is to be judged by the number of bodies in the parish church on Sunday morning. Just as the fear of the Lord is the beginning, but only the beginning, of wisdom, so physical presence at Mass, even the physical reception of the sacraments is only the beginning of a spiritual life. We need to develop that life in our potential undergraduates to a far higher degree than this.

In the end, I suppose, the acid test of our spiritual formation is the reality of our prayer-life, the extent to which we have developed an awareness of an order of reality transcending the world of immediate experience. This is what we must be aiming at all the time in our training of the young. Patiently, progressively, but without any dramatic forward leaps, we must be inculcating the habit of looking beyond the immediate present to the abiding realities, of seeing the wonder and glory of creation (which we are helping them to appreciate) as the reflection of eternal beauty and truth. All this, rarely explicit, will be implicit in so much of our teaching—provided we are ourselves steeped in the realization of it. Whether I am teaching English literature, musical appreciation or botany, I am inevitably to some extent getting my class to see what I see, to appreciate what I appreciate. My best pupils may outstrip me, while the worst ones will catch no more than a glimmer of what I am getting at. But to all of them I am giving something of myself. My technique as a teacher will be much the same as the technique of my secular colleagues or of pagan teachers in other establishments; the content of my lessons will be similar to the content of theirs. Yet, without necessarily mentioning explicitly any of my deepest convictions and certainly, let us hope, without dragging them in, I shall be having an effect different from that of anyone else, precisely because I am what I am.

It is, therefore, of the first importance that our own ideas about spirituality shall be sound if we are to have the right sort of spiritual effect on our pupils. Now I am certain that what we must aim at is a balanced, harmoniously integrated life in which, in St Ignatius' profound words, "we see God in his creatures and them *all* in him". This does not mean that we are for ever uttering exclamations of ecstatic wonder, or dragging spiritual allusions into our remarks or trying to show that Catholic writers are much better than any others (on the whole they are rather worse). It means that, while we have all the knowledge of, and enthusiasm for, our subject which the best of our secular colleagues have, while we are ambitious and rightly ambitious that our pupils shall succeed, while they see us wholly dedicated to their growth in wisdom, they realize too that this is far from being the whole story.

I should like to quote a brief passage from the sermon which Mgr Knox preached at Oxford when Campion Hall was celebrating its golden jubilee: "Historical truth, scientific truth, the method of philosophy, that delicate balance of mind which we call scholarship, are in themselves values that can claim our reverence; you can think of them as worth cultivating for their own sakes, although in fact the light which shines from them is not theirs; God is their Sun, and it is from him that their radiance is borrowed." True as that is, there is a subtle way in which it can be misunderstood as, indeed I believe, it often is misunderstood, by good people. You see, it is not that there is any contrast or conflict between the truth of God and the discoveries of man. The discoveries of man are discoveries of the truth of God in whatever field they are made. We are devoted to truth, dedicated to beauty, not relatively but absolutely. That is to say, I should not suggest or imply that I am interested in this topic *because* through it I learn more about God. I should not hint that I love beautiful things *because* they reveal God's beauty. Granted the need for ascetic discipline and self-restraint, the fact is that God's revelation is mediated to us through his creatures, and the more we know and love them for themselves, the more we come to know and love him.

"A balanced and harmoniously integrated life." If we enjoy this ourselves we shall not fail to lead our pupils towards that same goal. They will take with them into their universities our own love of truth, our own fastidious appreciation of beauty—truth that is many-sided, revealing God in his creation as the Son reveals himself in his incarnate life; beauty that is a reflection of the divine glory. Such fullness of life demands a personal response to God's glory in the practice of a genuine worship of him. The machinery is there—chaplaincies, sodalities, Catholic groups of one sort or another, which the undergraduate before coming up should be encouraged to support. But exhortation will avail nothing, and support will be perfunctory and ineffective, unless there is a personal sense of responsibility, a personal devotion to God revealing himself in his Church, as well as in the opportunities which he is giving the young person to grow up into a more complete person through the use of his God-given talents in a new world that is opening out.

CHAPTER XII

THE INTELLECTUAL FORMATION OF THE RELIGIOUS

It would hardly be unjust to claim that, until comparatively recently, the religious ideal presented to the nun could be summed up in the words of Charles Kingsley: "Be good, sweet maid, and let who will be clever." Nor, in fact, was this attitude of mind restricted merely to the Orders of women. I can well remember the days of my own early training, when the necessary business of study and the cultivation of intellectual interests was regarded as a serious threat to the purity of the ascetic doctrine one had imbibed in the noviceship. True, you could use the learning of Greek grammar as a subtler form of mortification, as a kind of spiritual hairshirt which did you good because it was a tedious exercise. But the awful danger attaching to so many subjects of study was that they might prove interesting for their own sakes; and that would never do. Anything "interesting for its own sake" was bound to be a distraction from God. Just as human love competed in our hearts with the love of God, so, apparently, human wisdom, human learning competed with the eternal truth and wisdom of God himself.

There has run through Christian history a curiously ambivalent attitude to learning, with the emphasis on the whole against the propriety or even permissibility of cultivating the things of the mind. We recall St Jerome's dream, in which he heard himself upbraided for being a Ciceronian and not a

Christian; we are all familiar with the incident in the life of St Thomas, when, as death approached, he saw all his accumulated store of learning as so much worthless straw; we all remember passages from À Kempis which leave us in little doubt what he thought of the learned; and so on.

Even such a cultivated and sensitive scholar as the late Mgr Knox was not, I think, entirely without scruple in all this. In a sermon which he preached on the occasion of the Jubilee of Campion Hall occur the following astringent words:

> Notoriously, there is no department of human learning which does not reckon Fathers of the Society of Jesus on the list of those whose labours have adorned it. Notoriously, there is no Order in the Church that cultivates so generously and utilizes so fruitfully the varied talent which is to be found among the members. But always, or so the world reasonably suspects, there is a hesitation, and *arrière penseé;* not learning as such, not art as such, but the glory of God as these can serve to promote it, is the object consciously envisaged. They will make, to be sure, a brilliant and varied contribution to the academic perfection of our institute, enriching it with the profound thought of a Rickaby, the political vision of a Charles Plater, the literary genius of a Hopkins. But all that will be, from their point of view, a by-product; sparks struck out incidentally from the anvil of a dedicated life. Predominantly, the Fathers of the Society are with us as university demonstrators, demonstrating what is, to flesh and blood, indemonstrable—that all our studies are, in a certain sense, toys; their subject-matter passes with the passage of time.

Now, of course, there is a sense in which all this is profoundly true and profoundly important. But there is a sense in which, I am absolutely convinced, it is disastrously misleading, a sense which has all too often bedevilled our efforts in the intellectual sphere and led our enemies to deride us as a Church of Philistines. For the inevitable implication of such a passage is that there is some necessary cleavage between the worship of God and the understanding of God's world, that learning is no part of true religion, although it may be a permissible activity, a harmless pursuit like playing golf (provided you do it for exercise and not because you enjoy it) or doing needlework (provided you are making vestments or at least producing tablemats to decorate the priest's parlour).

It is, then, hardly surprising that, in the first place, our attitude of mind gives scandal to the unbeliever. Some of you will be familiar with the passage from Teilhard de Chardin's *Milieu Divin:*

> Christianity, as some of the best of the Gentiles are inclined to think, is bad or inferior because it does not lead its followers to levels of attainment beyond ordinary human powers; rather it withdraws them from the ordinary ways of humankind and sets them on other paths It isolates them instead of merging them with the mass. Instead of harnessing them to the common task, it causes them to lose interest in it. If one of their religious or one of their priests should happen to devote his life to research in one of the so-called secular disciplines, he is very careful, as a rule, to point out that he is only lending himself for a time to serve a passing whim of scholarly fashion or even something ultimately of the stuff of illusion, and that simply in order to show that Christians are not, after all, the stupidest of men. When a Catholic works with us, we invariably get the impression that he is doing so in a spirit of condescension. He appears to be interested, but, in fact, because of his religion, he simply does not believe in the human effort as such. His heart is not really with us. Christianity nourishes deserters and false friends; that is what we cannot forgive.

We must all feel the genuine truth of that passage. But, unfortunate and serious as is the impression thus created on those outside the Church, what is still more serious is the effect on those who are, in sober fact, forced to lead an unnatural and almost schizophrenic existence. I am entirely convinced that immense psychological havoc has been created in far too many religious, and it is almost useless to talk about their intellectual formation until we have succeeded in clarifying our minds on this fundamental issue. Both superiors and subjects need to be convinced that the intellectual development of the latter is just as truly a part of their growth in religious perfection as are the conventional exercises of piety or the recognized ascetic practices to which we are introduced in the early days of our religious life.

In theory, there ought not to be the slightest problem. We readily accept the definition of man as a rational animal but, in practice, all too often think of human perfection largely in terms of training the animal side of our nature and letting the rational element look after itself. We spend hours, months, perhaps years in the business of developing certain religious mannerisms, deportment and so on, and tend to regard religious perfection as consisting in a combination of these externals with a certain degree of proficiency in one or two standard virtues. It is only in recent years, under pressure from examining boards and, let us admit it, because we are anxious to save the money which we should otherwise have to spend on the salaries of secular mistresses, that we have taken to sending our younger nuns to the universities or the training colleges. But it is all a regrettable interruption, a grave distraction from the simple religious life as outlined to us in the works of Alphonsus Rodriguez, who presents the Fathers of the Desert—the Desert, forsooth!—as the prototypes of the authentic religious, plunged, by Divine Providence, into the crowded cities of our twentieth century.

As I say, the theory is simple and obvious enough. God is the source of all truth, the very power of thinking that lies behind all thought. In every new aspect of truth that we glimpse, we touch the hem of his garment, just as truly as when we perform some act of virtue or lose ourselves in the peace of meditative prayer. Since God is the Supreme Spirit it is by virtue of the development of our spiritual qualities, not least of our intellect, that we grow more like him. Not, indeed, in selfish withdrawal to some ivory tower, aloof from our fellow-mortals. God does not want us to become dilettantes or aesthetes; but equally he does not want us to bury in napkins such intellectual abilities as we may possess. When St Paul talks of the "folly of the Cross", he is not preaching a doctrine of the worship of God through stupidity. How can we worship Infinite Wisdom save by the proper use of our own wisdom?

Yet, as I have already said, there is in the long history of Christian experience so much emphasis on the playing-down of the intellect, almost on a cult of the unintelligent, that we must now investigate the process by which this misunderstanding of the plain truth has come about.

It goes back to the very circumstances of the incarnation itself. In becoming man, our Lord involved himself in what we may term an unintellectual milieu, lived an unintellectual life among unintellectual people. In the same way, he involved himself in a *Jewish* milieu, in a primitive, semi-pastoral milieu, in a country where men wore a certain kind of clothing, ate certain kinds of food and so on. But all these were the *accidents* of the incarnation, having nothing at all to do with its essential purpose and its essential message. Not only was the individual quality of his social background, with all that that meant of manners of behaving, forms of thought and speech, style of living and the rest uniquely *his,* in a way which cannot be shared by the vast majority of his followers, but the shaping of his individual mind was conditioned by factors, many of which have disappeared from history.

All this means that Christianity, in one aspect, has about it a certain flavour of the remote past; unless we are careful, our practice of it almost becomes a study in archaeology. The responsibility of the Christian is to make sure that this does not happen, that while our religion is necessarily linked with and indeed based on certain historic moments in the past, it is none the less of today and tomorrow. It is not fidelity to, it is a betrayal of the incarnation itself if we do not see the continuing development of man's thought and achievement as an extension of the incarnation, in that it is an extension of man himself. Each of us, in fulfilling his or her intellectual nature, is adding to the stature of man himself, and is thereby continuing that development of all mankind which makes possible the fuller achievement of God-in-man.

This ought to be so obvious as to need no stressing. Yet the sad truth is that, for a variety of reasons which I now propose to investigate, Christianity in general, and the Catholic Church in particular, have increasingly come to be regarded by the learned world as unintellectual, if not positively hostile to the things of the mind. We point indignantly to the great names of the past of those who have managed to combine faith with scientific or philosophical or scholarly interests; but I am not sure that the instinct of the learned world is altogether unsound. We do not, as a body, regard intellectual or artistic achievement as something desirable for its own sake. Why is this?

In the first place, though again for purely accidental reasons, the early Christians found themselves in direct opposition to contemporary paganism, in which religion and letters were inextricably commingled. Inside and outside Judaism, Christianity made its first converts very largely from among the simple and unlettered, so that there seemed to be a sort of universal validity attaching to the text: "Thou hast hidden all this from the wise and prudent, and revealed it to little children." Forgetting that their founder was incarnate wisdom, these early Christians developed a kind of inferiority feeling towards their intellectual contemporaries, and by a not uncommon psychological reaction tended to denigrate the qualities which were not conspicuously present in their own ranks, but were to be found in plenty among the pagans. Just as it was perhaps necessary for ultimate sanity that the Fathers of the Desert should make their extravagant protest against the normal decencies of civilized living, so perhaps it was inevitable that in the early centuries of Christian growth paganism could be resisted satisfactorily only by an out-and-out condemnation even of those qualities in it which were of value. This is no justification for maintaining a similar Philistinism down to our own day. As we have already seen, that great scholar St Jerome clearly had twinges of conscience about his literary taste, not apparently realizing that it was this gift which enabled him to give to the Church the great legacy of his translation of the Bible.

I am inclined to suspect that, just as in the material sphere the Church was plagued by a Manichean reluctance to admit wholeheartedly that the human body and the whole range of physical beauty are just as much a product of the creative love of God as are the angelic intelligences, so, in the spiritual order, it was felt that there was some kind of dichotomy, a division of truth into those truths that matter, the object of theological investigation, and unimportant or worldly truths, the object of scientific or literary study. True as it is that the great monastic houses were preserving for posterity some of the literary masterpieces of classical antiquity, I hope I am not being unjust in supposing that the monks were given the job of copying out manuscripts to keep them out of mischief. Their real work was the Divine Office—the *Opus Dei;* everything else was a way of filling in the time between the Canonical Hours.

This dichotomy between the different levels of truth is reflected in the debate which marked, possibly disfigured, the development of medieval philosophy. The idea of wedding pagan philosophy with Christian theology was one which saints like Bernard and Peter Damian found shocking. When in the course of this debate St Bernard said: *Non in dialectica complacuit Deo salvare populum suum,* he was scoring a debating point. His words should not be taken as expressing a profound truth of general application. Yet, although the great Dominicans of the thirteenth century, St Albert and St Thomas, did achieve a temporary success, and laid the foundations of a genuine synthesis of human learning and divine revelation, the later Middle Ages were marked by a fear of, and hostility to, scientific investigation and the use of reason outside a very narrow framework. We may, in passing, derive what comfort we like from the fact that it was Luther who went to the greatest lengths in the denigration of reason, of which he said that "it could only blaspheme and dishonour everything that God has done".

The outcome of all this was the Renaissance, the rise of rationalism and the increasing secularization of literature, science, philosophy, art and culture as a whole. This is the world into which we are born; this is the world we are called upon to redeem. The world into which Christ was born was the world of Judaism. He redeemed it, not by rejecting it but by developing its basic truths, by integrating it into a fuller world-picture. "I come not to destroy" he said, "but to fulfil." We can, it seems to me, take the same words to describe our own task.

Some readers may be feeling by now a sense of frustration. They came to this chapter, perhaps, hoping for a cut-and-dried scheme, a syllabus, a curriculum. And here I am talking generalities and indulging in historical investigations and the like. Yet I am convinced that every word I have said is not merely relevant, it is essential to a proper understanding of what is meant by intellectual formation in our present context. Turning then to our immediate purpose, I should like to stress, first of all, that we must see our intellectual formation not as something of purely secondary importance, still less as something at variance with our religious formation; we must see it as an integral part of our whole spiritual perfection.

We so easily fall victims to the completely false idea that there is a kind of timeless pattern or scheme of religious perfection, consisting largely of a set of negative attitudes. Poverty means not merely owning nothing, but regarding all material creatures as *there* to be "given up". Chastity means not just dedicating ourselves to God by renouncing marriage, but regarding marriage itself as a rather regrettable institution; obedience means not just finding God's will in my superior's decisions, but having no sort of preference or inclinations of my own. In so far as the ideal religious perfection has a positive content this is to be found in the performance of a few simple tasks, in surroundings as remote as possible from our fellow-men, although, to be sure, we need some of these to exercise our charity on. If we were to be asked what we regarded as the ideal religious situation, we should probably think we ought to say: "Carthusian life" or "Carmel".

But the plain truth is that the ideal religious situation is the situation in which each of us finds himself or herself. For our Lord, the ideal situation was, for most of his life, Nazareth; but this does not mean that carpenters as a body are dearer to God than any other group of men. For the member of a teaching Order, the ideal situation is the class-room or the lecture-room, the laboratory or the library, every bit as much as the chapel or the cloister. We redeem our world, our generation, by immersing ourselves in it, by acting upon it like leaven, by restoring to what may have *become* "purely secular" that element of the supernatural which it is at once our privilege and our duty to contribute. Strictly speaking, of course, there is nothing secular, since everything comes from the hand of God, is sustained by him and, further, is a feature of that world which was, in principle, sanctified and supernaturalized by the human activities of God-made man.

Those among us who are superiors should reflect that their chief motive in setting aside subjects for further study should be, not that the Order needs educated members, true and important as that undoubtedly is; not, again, because we need someone to teach history or mathematics or chemistry in this or that school, though this is an obvious factor in our selection; our first motive should be our duty to our subjects. We have the responsibility of seeing that the unique qualities which each of them possesses are developed to the full. Each of them is an individual, uniquely dear to God and to be uniquely cherished by me, her superior, standing to her in the place of God.

This is the ideal. In practice, of course, in this imperfect world I may have to send someone to study biology who would be happier studying modern languages or music, because the immediate needs of the Province demand this. This will give any number of opportunities for exercising detachment and other official virtues. But I should be happier to see my subjects grow and develop in their more natural surroundings, just as I rejoice to see the plants and flowers of God's creation blossom and mature.

If, whether as subject or superior, I have the opportunity for pursuing intellectual interests, I must, with complete unselfconsciousness, rejoice in the exercise of the talents that God has given me.

"In the beginning was the Word"—the perfect expression and utterance of the truth of God. Uttered in eternity, that Word finds expression in time in every aspect of created truth. Whatever be the truth I am concerned with, I am, in a real sense, listening to the same Word of God. How can I ever doubt that my intellectual activities and achievements are just as truly a part of my sanctification as any other? "Be ye perfect as your heavenly Father is perfect"—perfect in all wisdom and truth, as he is perfect in goodness and love.

By a strange anomaly, and for reasons which we have already glanced at, it is an undeniable fact that intellectual progress at every level has been achieved in the modern world almost entirely by men who are agnostic and formally irreligious. Yet, albeit unconsciously, their achievement has made a genuine contribution to our own religious outlook. If today we have a greater and more awe-inspiring sense of the grandeur and majesty of God's creation, it is because of the discoveries of men who give no thought to its creator. We owe them a debt, a debt which we can best repay by enabling them to see that their splendid vision takes on a new splendour when it is related to the fuller truth which we possess by faith. For their sakes no less than for our own, we should enlarge our minds as much as may be, knowing that whatever addition is made to the sum of human knowledge and human understanding, is a further addition to our appreciation of the totality of truth.

SELECT BIBLIOGRAPHY

Bouyer, Louis: *Christian Humanism,* trans. by A. V. Littledale, Westminster, Md., Newman, 1958.

Brinton, Crane: *Ideas and Men,* Englewood Cliffs, N.J., Prentice-Hall, 1950.

Caponigri, A. Robert: *Modern Catholic Thinkers: An Anthology,* introduction by Martin C. D'Arcy, S.J., New York, Regnery and London, Burns and Oates, 1960.

Dawson, Christopher: *The Dividing of Christendom,* New York, Sheed & Ward, 1965.

De Lubac, Henri: *Teilhard de Chardin: The Man and His Meaning,* New York, Hawthorn Books, 1965.

Goldbrunner, Josef: *Holiness Is Wholeness and Other Essays,* Notre Dame, Ind., University of Notre Dame Press, 1964.

Hofinger, Johannes, S.J.: *The Art of Teaching Christian Doctrine,* Notre Dame, Ind., University of Notre Dame Press, 1962.

Jankauskas, John J.: *Our Tongues Were Loosed,* Westminster, Md., Newman, 1965.

Jaeger, Werner: *Humanism and Theology,* Milwaukee, Wis., Marquette University Press, 1945.

Link, Mark J., S.J.: *Christ Teaches Us Today,* Chicago, Loyola University Press, 1965.

Rahner, Karl, S.J.: *The Christian Commitment,* New York, Sheed & Ward, 1965.

Teilhard, de Chardin, Pierre: *Hymn of the Universe,* New York, Harper & Row, 1965.

Wolf, Donald J., and Schall, James V., S.J. (eds.): *Current Trends in Theology,* New York, Doubleday, 1965.